Reconstructing the Christ Symbol

Essays in Feminist Christology

Edited by
MARYANNE STEVENS

PAULIST PRESS
New York/Mahwah

Library of Congress Cataloging-in-Publication Data

Reconstructing the Christ symbol: essays in feminist christology/edited by
Maryanne Stevens.
    p.   cm.
    Includes bibliographical references.
    ISBN 0-8091-3439-X
    1. Jesus Christ—Person and offices. 2. Feminist theology. I. Stevens,
Maryanne, 1948-
BT205.R34   1993
232'.082—dc20   93-38018
                                                             CIP

Published by Paulist Press
997 Macarthur Boulevard
Mahwah, N.J. 07430

Printed and bound in the United States of America

Contents

Introduction

MARYANNE STEVENS

Pervading the symbolism of the Christian churches and foundational to the understanding of sacrament, pastoral practice and church law is the image of Christ. Therefore the use of predominantly white male imagery to present Christ has far-reaching implications for those excluded from stereotypical Western male understandings and imagery. For example, African Americans were often taught that following Jesus meant docility, meekness and idleness in the face of racial oppression. Jesus was honored when they accepted their roles as servants in society. And, for women, Jesus' male gender has been construed to mean they are to subject themselves to male authority, for God chose to reveal *himself* in a male person—Jesus the God-*man*. Feminist theologians argue that the very credibility of the Christian tradition rests on an understanding of Jesus as one who proclaimed the iconoclastic reversal of status systems, especially the status systems within religious bodies. Thus, the Christ symbol must be reconstructed so that all who engage it may find in it a source of human liberation.

Although neither blacks nor women are as systematically denigrated and excluded by religious thought today as they have been throughout Christian history, many Christian churches continue to resist this reconstruction. In 1976 the Roman Catholic Congregation for the

Doctrine of the Faith reiterated the traditional arguments against the participation of women in all ministries in the church. In its *Declaration Concerning the Question of the Admission of Women to the Ministerial Priesthood,* the Congregation argued that priestly ordination be reserved to men because:

> [T]he priest in his ministry represents Christ, especially in the eucharist when he acts in the very person of Christ. The priest in the specific and unique act of presiding at the eucharist is a sacramental sign in and through which the presence of Christ, who was and remains a man, is shown forth. This is in accord with the nature of sacramental signification, which requires that there be a natural resemblance between the sign and the person or thing signified.[1]

Clearly, Jesus was a first century Jewish male. But need the resurrected Christ be presented only as male? Or is this merely the ugly head of patriarchy continuing to pervade and thus distort our religious symbolism?

In April, 1992, the theology department of Creighton University joined with the university's Center for the Study of Religion and Society and university college to sponsor a symposium on this question. The symposium was titled "Who Do You Say That I Am? Christology in Women's Voices." Women scholars from a variety of Christian traditions representing the Hispanic, Asian and Afro-American and white cultures were invited to present their work and engage participants in discussion. Karl Rahner argued that it is the task "of the church of women," supported by the "message of the Gospel and the power of the Spirit," not "the church of officialdom" to provide "the concrete model, the constructive pattern of life which is necessary for women in the present age." This task "cannot be taken away by the official authorities."[2] These essays provide a look at what the church of women has done to reconstruct the symbol of Christ so that it might further provide the impetus for all Christian women and men to respond to the liberating work to which we are called.

Keynoter Rosemary Ruether calls for Christology to manifest the universality and inclusivity Christ proclaimed in redeeming us from the bondage to sin that is the universal human dilemma. Warning of a new church-world split, Ruether argues that if women are recognized as fully human within the world, an egalitarian anthropology should also pervade the church. The patriarchal anthropology informing our understandings of Christ not only excludes women from equality of leadership in the church, it distorts the understanding of what a disciple of Jesus should be. As Christians we are followers of Jesus' way. He is the foundational representative of this way of the cross and liberation. He is not its exclusive possibility.

Rita Brock encourages us to return to the story of the Jesus movement looking for a new message of hope. In her experiences of feminist work on child abuse and her struggles to live in our society as a mixed-race Asian American woman, Brock has found the image of Jesus as the lamb slain for our redemption functioning to support a concept of power and obedience to authority that is dehumanizing rather than liberating. Traditional Christology resting on this image of the docile, obedient, innocent servant has often advised victims to be self-sacrificing and forgiving of their oppressors. Brock's challenge is to shift our interpretations of Christianity's origins to uncover the radical stubbornness and willfulness of Jesus in the face of intimidation. This reinterpretation is of the utmost necessity when we live in a society and within churches that seek to make us passive and acquiescent.

Jacquelyn Grant's thesis also critiques the use of the servant image of Christ and calls for a reconstruction of the Christ symbol from the interplay of social context, scripture, and traditions. Focusing on the black woman as one who concretely shares the suffering of Christ through the triadic oppression of race, sex, and economics, Grant's understanding of Jesus includes his identification as stranger, outcast, hungry, weak, and poor. Just as African American women can find in the reconstructed Christ a source of liberation so Christ can be liberated from the oppressions of patriarchy, white supremacy, and class privilege by the insights of black women.

Marina Herrera, sensitive to the understandings of Christianity that led to the extermination of the Native Americans, resists the category "feminist" because she is concerned that it too narrowly focuses our energies on only the liberation of women. She prefers to name herself an "Americanist." She calls for a critique of all things European, including the blond, blue-eyed Jesus, using the prism of the diversity unique to this continent. Herrera argues that our images of Christ will be reconstructed only as we recast our images of one another as men and women, as white and black, as Polish or African or Hispanic.

Elizabeth Johnson proposes the powerful female figure of Wisdom, *Sophia* in Greek, as a helpful corrective to the androcentric bias of traditional Christology. The wisdom tradition, if critically retrieved, can yield an inclusive vision of wholeness beneficial not only to women, but also to men and the earth. Johnson shows how the fluidity of gender symbolism in Jesus-*Sophia* breaks with the fixation on the maleness of Jesus and how the use of the *Sophia* image can contribute to a praxis centered on justice for the poor, respectful encounter with world religions and ecological care for the earth.

Finally, Eleanor McLaughlin illustrates through a review of the tradition, the body-denying androcentrism in Christology and calls for a symbolic way to acknowledge Jesus as a person whom we can experience as either man or woman. Using the literary critical paradigm of the transvestite, the cross-dresser, she presents Jesus as the trickster who dismantles our categories and peels us open to new depths of humanity, divinity, femaleness, and maleness. Just as Jesus flew in the face of the culture, McLaughlin calls for women's ordination (a woman's body in sacred space, a woman dressed as a man dressed as a woman) to reshape the categories of classical Christology.

These essays are offered to readers as "merely hints and guesses, hints followed by guesses...the rest is prayer, observance, discipline, thought, and action."[3] Neither the symposium nor these published essays would have been possible without the help of Creighton's Center for the Study of Religion and Society and Michael Proterra, S.J., Dean of Creighton's College of Arts and Sciences. Sincere thank-yous are expressed to them and to Maryellen Read without whom this manuscript could not have been presented in a readable form.

Notes

1. Congregation for the Doctrine of the Faith, *Inter Insigniores* (Oct. 15, 1976) AAS 69(1977): 98-116.

2. Karl Rahner, "The Position of Woman in the New Situation in which the Church Finds Herself," *Theological Investigations,* v. 8, trans. David Bourke (New York: Herder and Herder, 1971).

3. T.S. Eliot, *The Four Quartets* (London: Faber and Faber, 1960), lines 212-213.

Can Christology Be Liberated From Patriarchy?

ROSEMARY RADFORD RUETHER

In recent Vatican and Roman Catholic episcopal statements, Christology is used as the keystone of the argument against women's ordination. It is said that women, by their very nature, cannot represent Christ. Therefore they cannot be priests, since priests "represent" Christ.[1] This argument has been echoed in other high church statements, Anglican, Lutheran, and Eastern Orthodox. What is the meaning of this use of Christology against women's full participation in the Christian Church? If women cannot represent Christ, in what sense can it be said that Christ represents women? Does this mean that Christ does not redeem women, but reinforces women's bondage in a patriarchal social system? If this is the case, shouldn't women who seek liberation from patriarchy reject Christianity?

Traditionally, it has been claimed that Christ is the redeemer and representative of all humanity. He is the one who overcomes the bondage to sin that is the universal human dilemma. Thus, it would seem that the symbols the Christian Church uses to express Christology should also manifest universality and inclusivity. These symbols should embrace the authentic humanness and fulfilled hopes of all persons. How is it possible that more than one-half of humanity, more than half of the membership of the

Christian churches themselves, find themselves rendered inferior and excluded by Christology?

In this essay I wish to examine the development of the Christological symbols and how they have been shaped by an androcentric ideology that becomes explicit when they are used to exclude women from representation of Christ. I will then ask whether Christology can be liberated from this androcentric bias and become genuinely inclusive of women.

The history of Christological symbols

Early Christianity used the word *Logos* to define the presence of God made incarnate in Jesus the Christ. This term drew on a long tradition of religious philosophy. In Greek and Hellenistic Jewish philosophy, the divine *Logos* was the means by which the transcendent God came forth in the beginning to shape the visible cosmos. The *Logos* was simultaneously the immanence of God and the ground of the visible cosmos. In Hellenistic Jewish terms, the *Logos* of *Sophia* (Wisdom) was God's self-manifestation by which God created the world, providentially guided it, was revealed to it, and through whom the world was reconciled to God.

The *Logos* was particularly identified with the rational principle in each human soul. By linking the term "Christ" (Messiah), through whom God redeemed the world, to the *Logos* as the creational principle, early Christianity prevented a split between redemption and creation that was threatened by gnosticism. Christians affirmed that the God revealed in Jesus Christ was the same God who created the world in the beginning. Christ was the authentic ground of creation, manifest in fulfilled form, over against the alienation of creation from its true being. This concept of the *Logos* as the divine identity of Christ would seem to be inclusive of women, pointing all humans, male and female, to the foundation of their true humanness.[2]

But this Hellenistic philosophical tradition was also shaped in a patriarchal culture which gave the term *Logos* and "Christ" an androcentric bias. Since divinity, sovereign power, rationality, and normative humanity were all assumed by this culture to be male, all the theological reference points for defining Christ were defined androcentrically. Normative humanity, the image of God in "man," and the divine *Logos* were interlocking androcentric concepts in the theological definition of Christ, reinforcing the assumption that God is male, and that the human Christ must be a male in order to reveal the male God.

Christianity has never said that God was literally male, but it has assumed that God represents preeminently the qualities of rationality and sovereign power. Since men were assumed to be rational, and women less so or not at all, and men exercised the public power normally denied to women, the male metaphor was seen as appropriate for God, while female metaphors for God came to be regarded as inappropriate and indeed "pagan." The *Logos* who reveals the "Father," therefore, was presumed to be properly represented as male, even though the Jewish Wisdom tradition had used the female metaphor, *Sophia,* for this same idea. The maleness of the historical Jesus undoubtedly reinforced this preference for male-identified metaphors, such as *Logos* and "Son of God," over the female metaphor of *Sophia.*

Within Trinitarian theology, to term the *Logos* or Second Person of the Trinity as the "Son" is odd and misleading, since it suggests a subordinate and derivative status of the *Logos,* as the male child is "begotten" by, and under the power of, his Father. This "Son-Father" metaphor is used to represent the immanence of God as "under" and derivative from divine transcendence. Taken literally, these metaphors reinforce the maleness of God in both aspects, and set up a patriarchal relationship between the two "persons" of God.

These notions of the maleness of God also affect the interpretation of the concept of *imago Dei*. Genesis 1:27-8 says: "So God created man (Adam) in his own image, in the image of God he created him, male and female he (they) created them." This formula, with its plural collective term for God, leaves open the possibility that the human thus created is to be understood generically, and that Genesis 27b teaches that the image of God is possessed by both male and female. This would mean that woman shares in the stewardship over creation referred to in Genesis 1:26.[3]

However, most of the patristic and medieval tradition rejected the possibility that women were equally theomorphic.[4] In most interpretations, the concept of *imago Dei* was distinguished from gender difference. One way to interpret this distinction was to make the *imago Dei* asexually spiritual, neither male nor female. Gender difference then referred to the bodily characteristics which humans share with animals but not with God. Following Philo, some church fathers saw gender appearing only in the fallen state of "man." Gregory of Nyssa read the text in this way.[5]

St. Augustine drew a different conclusion. For him, it was the male who possessed the image of God normatively, while women were included only "under the male" as their head. In themselves, women did not possess the image of God, but were the image of the bodily creation which the human male was given to rule over.[6] Such an interpretation of the image of God reflects the patriarchal legal and social order in which the *paterfamilias* or male head of the family was the corporate head and representative of the whole *familia*—women, children, slaves, animals, and land under his control. The male head alone possessed personhood juridically in the public order.

Augustine and the other church fathers never denied that women have redeemable souls. Nevertheless, they believed that women in their specific femaleness—psychic and bodily—were the opposite of the divine. They reflected bodily, creaturely reality. The idea of woman as body takes for granted the androcentric perspective of the male as the one who "looks at" woman, controlling and defining her as bodily object. The male is "mind" or subject, and the woman is body or object. Woman's own experience of herself as subject is not taken into account in this definition.

This androcentric view of woman as object allowed the church fathers to ignore the contradiction between woman's possession of a redeemable soul, and her lack of the status of *imago Dei* in her own right. This concept of women lacking full personhood, as an image of God only derivatively, was reinforced by the scholastic appropriation of Aristotelian biology. This (false) biology asserted that the male alone provides the seed or "form" of the offspring, while the female contributes only the material substratum which is formed.[7] If this process is fully carried out, and the male seed fully forms the female matter, another male will be born. Females are the result of a defect in gestation in which the maternal matter fails to be fully formed by the male seed. In this construct of male to female as form to matter (which denies the existence of the female ovum), the female is defined as a defective human, lacking in full humanity, inferior in bodily strength, adequate rationality, and moral self-control. These defects preclude both autonomy and rule over others for females, and demand that the woman be subject to the male.

The female then, was defined by medieval theologians such as Thomas Aquinas, who appropriated this

Aristotelian view, as a non-normative human who lacks the fullness of human nature. The male is the "perfect" or complete expression of the human species. Aquinas concluded from this anthropology that the maleness of the historical Jesus was an ontological necessity, not a historical accident. In order for Jesus as the Christ to represent humanity as a whole, he must be male, because only the male possesses the fullness of human nature. The female cannot represent the human, either for herself or generically.[8]

This interlocking set of ideas about the maleness of God, the *Logos* of God, the *imago Dei*, and Christ threaten to undermine the basic Christian belief that women are included in the redemption of "man" won by Christ. The church fathers assumed that she was included, while being humanly non-normative and non-theomorphic, because they assumed a patriarchal ideology in which women were included "under" an ontological maleness theologically, just as they were included "under," and represented by, the male head of the family juridically in patriarchal society and law.

Today women have won the right of citizens or "civil persons" in the political-juridical order. Higher education, opened to women, has disproved the notion of women's inferior intelligence. Aristotelian biology has been proven false. Indeed, the actual gestation of the child proceeds in the opposite way, with the female ovum and uterus shaping a female generic fetus, from which a differentiation process must take place in order to make a male.[9] All the androcentric assumptions on which past Christological symbols were based have been thrown into question.

Today a Christology which elevates Jesus' human maleness to ontologically necessary significance makes the Christ symbol non-inclusive of women. In order to reaffirm the basic Christian belief that women are included in redemption, "in Christ," all the symbolic underpinnings of Christology must be reinterpreted. Is this possible? What might this mean? In order to reassess the relationship of Christology and gender, we might start by examining the more gender inclusive possibilities of the basic symbols of God and the image of God, Christ, and the *Logos* of God, on which Christology was built. We should also ask about Jesus' own teaching and praxis.

Jewish understandings and Jesus' praxis

Jewish tradition thinks of God as beyond gender. God is thought of as both a ruler and a parent. This divine ruler-parent sometimes exercises power in wrathful and judgmental ways, but, at other times, he can be thought of as merciful, forgiving, compassionate, and even as patient and long-suffering. In terms of gender stereotypes, God is androgynous. Sometimes female metaphors are explicitly used for these "maternal" aspects of God.[10] However, since the male pronoun is used for God, this might suggest that God is an androgynous male.

But Judaism also rejects literalism about verbal or visual images used for God. God is beyond all such creaturely images, and to take any image literally is idolatry. In order to combine these two insights—God's "androgynous" nature and yet transcendence of all anthropomorphic literalism—we must become clearer about the metaphorical character of such gender images. In God's self, God is neither male nor female (or humanly gendered at all). But our metaphors for God must include both male and female. This cannot be done simply by adding together patriarchal masculine and feminine gender stereotypes, or even by giving a male God a "feminine" side, for this still leaves women without full humanity.

We must use gender symbols to affirm that God both

transcends and yet includes the fullness of the humanity of both men and women. Women must gain their "male side" in relation to God, as historically men were allowed to gain their "female side" through the androgynous "motherly father." Only then can we say that both men and women possess the image of God in mutuality, and yet also as full persons in their own right. To simply include women under a male "head," or to include women as complementary parts of a whole found only as the heterosexual couple, is not sufficient.

Another way the Hebrew tradition brought androgyny into God was to picture the immanence of God in female metaphors. The most notable of these is the "Wisdom" metaphor. Wisdom caring for the cosmos is pictured as a woman caring for her household.[11] This Wisdom idea is of particular significance for Christians, because theologically Wisdom plays the same roles as the *Logos* (and was the original version of this idea). She is the presence of God as means of creation, relation, and redemption. Jesus' divinity is sometimes identified as the "Wisdom" of God.[12]

Recognition of the Wisdom version of this concept deliteralizes metaphors for the second person of the Trinity, revealed in Christ as "Son of God." The idea that the immanence of God is like a "son," or male offspring, in relation to a genitor, or "father," cannot be taken literally. God as *Logos-Sophia* is neither male nor female, and can be represented in both male and female metaphors. We must also ask whether the parent-child metaphor, for imaging the relation of divine transcendence and immanence, needs to be discarded as more misleading than revealing.

But surely, one might say, the Jewish notion of Messiah was always and only a male! The Messiah idea originated as a title for the kings of Israel and later as the ideal and future King of Israel.[13] Although rulers, representing divine sovereignty, were generally thought of as male, female rulers were not unknown in the ancient Middle East. Jesus' own preferred title for the *Coming One* (whom he probably did not identify with himself) was *ben Adam*, usually translated "Son of Man." This term, drawn from the Book of Daniel and other apocalyptic literature, sees the Messiah as the collective expression of Israel, itself the representative of corporate humanity.

In Jewish liturgy *ben Adam* refers to females, as well as to males, despite its androcentric form. Since generic humanity cannot today be seen as normatively male, a more accurate translation of this term would be "The Human One." This is the way the *Inclusive Language Lectionary,* prepared by the National Council of Churches of Christ of the U.S.A., chose to translate this term for liturgical reading of Scripture.[14]

From an examination of the symbols used for Christ, we turn to the praxis of the historical Jesus, as interpreted in the gospels. Here we see the figure of an iconoclastic prophet of God who stands in judgment on social and religious systems which exclude subordinated and marginated people from divine favor. Jesus' mission is seen as one of bringing "good news to the poor," hope to despised people whom the priestly and clerical classes regarded as unworthy of redemption. Jesus' prophetic praxis confronts these male leaders for their pretenses of special privilege with God, and for their exclusion of the unlearned and the "unclean."

Rather than these male leaders, it is often women among the despised groups who are able to hear God's prophetic word and be converted. Because women were at the bottom of those systems of privilege decried in the gospel stories, they became the representatives of the "last who shall be first in the Kingdom of God." Luke, in the

Magnificat, makes Jesus' mother, Mary, potentially despised as one whose child is not her husband's, the exemplar of the messianic community. She is the servant of God who will be lifted up, while the mighty of the world are put down from their thrones.[15]

All four gospels tell the Jesus story as a drama of mounting conflict in which the messianic prophet is rejected, first by his family and hometown folk, then by the religious leaders, then by the crowd of his popular followers, and then by his own male disciples. It is the core group of his female followers who remain faithful at the cross and are first at the tomb. They are the first witnesses of the Resurrection. They are commissioned by the Risen Lord to take the good news back to the male disciples huddled in the upper room.[16]

Scholars have rejected this "empty tomb" story as secondary and unhistorical.[17] But they have failed to ask the question of why all four gospels tell the story in this way. Is it not to make dramatically clear that despised women, last in the present social and religious order, are the faithful remnant who are first in the redeemed order?

Luke also includes women in his account of Pentecost. Luke uses the text of the prophet Joel to buttress his story of the restoration of the prophetic Spirit to the messianic community, in which the Spirit is given to the "men servants and the maid servants," and "your sons and your daughters shall prophesy."[18] This inclusion of women reflects the fact that women were included in the prophetic office in Hebrew Scripture, as well as in early Christianity.[19] The late second century church order, the *Didache*, shows that there were still Christians in that period who saw the prophet as the normative church leader.[20]

Christianity through the ages

Despite these didactic patterns of early Christianity which saw the messianic community as overturning established hierarchies and including women as the first believers, first witnesses and prophetic spokespersons of the Risen Lord, it is not clear how much impact such patterns had on early Christian social practice. We get only glimpses of some ministry of women that seems quickly suppressed by an insurgent patriarchal concept of the church.[21] Why did this happen?

I suggest that one clue to this repression of women lies in the ambivalent understanding of the church as messianic community. One group of early Christians understood this apocalyptically, as an impending end of this present world, terminating its mortality and need for reproductive renewal. For them, women had been liberated from traditional gender roles by Christ, since both male and female Christians belonged to a transcendent, heavenly order where marriage and reproduction would be no longer necessary.[22]

The insurgent patriarchal Christianity of the deutero-Pauline tradition repressed both the apocalypticism and the incipient egalitarianism of this eschatological interpretation of the church. These churchmen were the authors of the church's historical survival and institutionalization. But they also reaffirmed the patriarchal, slave-holding social order as still normative for Christian society. The new freedom of women to travel as itinerant preachers, freed by Christ from marriage, was repressed in favor of a Christianity that declared women second in creation, first in sin, silent in church, and saved by childbearing.[23]

The conflict between egalitarian, eschatological Christianity and patriarchal, historical Christianity continued in the second and third centuries in the gnostic and

Montanist struggles.[24] It was resolved in the late fourth to sixth centuries in a new synthesis of the two. In this new synthesis, the eschatological ideal of chastity was shorn of its egalitarianism and began to incorporate the patriarchal, clerical leadership class.[25] Marriage, as the lifestyle of most Christians, was reaffirmed, but as a second class, lay stratum of the church.[26]

From the fourth to the ninth century, celibate women were gradually deprived of the remnants of pastoral ministry and segregated into convents under male episcopal control.[27] The patriarchal, hierarchical church leadership was then incorporated into the Roman Empire as new agents of its rule. This fourth century synthesis of patriarchal, imperial church organization, together with a clericalized monastic counter-culture, became normative Christianity for the next thousand years. Yet a resistance to it from both celibate women and married clerics continued through the Middle Ages.[28]

The Reformation

The Reformation represented a revolt against clerical celibacy. It restored the married clergy, but went on to abolish monasteries for men or women.[29] This meant that it rooted itself all the more exclusively in the patriarchal type of Christianity. The patriarchal family is now stressed as the nucleus of the church, modeled by the married pastor and his obedient wife and children. The household codes become the norm for Christian society with a new force.[30]

However, the eschatological counter-culture did not disappear with the suppression of monasticism. Rather it returned in its more radical form, in mystical and millenialist sects who again saw the church as a messianic community living in the last days of world history. They anticipated the coming Kingdom by withdrawing from the evil structures of the worldly society and its church. Some of these sects rediscovered the early Christian idea that the redeemed had transcended the patriarchal order of history. Freed from gender roles, men and women "saints" became equal in a new redemptive society. Women again were mandated to preach and prophesy "in the Spirit." Some also rediscovered gnostic ideas of divine androgyny.[31]

We have here two different lines of Christianity which lend themselves to different Christologies. Patriarchal Christianity moves toward the integration of the Lordship of Christ with the lordship of Caesar. Christ as divine *Logos* is the apex of a hierarchical social-political order baptized as Christendom. As delegate of the heavenly Father, Christ rules over the cosmos and is, in turn, the source of the ecclesiastical and political hierarchies of church and state.[32] On the familial and personal level, Christ mandates the headship of husband over wife, and the rule of reason over the body. Women as wives, as laity and as subjects of monarchs, under the rule of their husbands, represent the bodily realm that is to be ruled over by the male Christological principle in each system of dominance and subjugation.

In the mystical and millenialist Christologies, by contrast, Christ is the transcendent ground of being for the redeemed who have departed from this fallen world and its corrupt social systems, and are both awaiting and anticipating a redeemed order beyond this world. For some of these sects, Christ is asexual and spiritually androgynous. He encompasses both men and women on a level transcendent to the separation into genders and reproductive roles that happened through the Fall, restoring the redeemed to their prelapsarian unity.

The redeemed participate in the eschatological new life in Christ by putting aside sexual activity and reproduction. Thereby they recover the sinless and spiritually androgynous mode of being before the fall into sin and death, which necessitated gender, sex, and reproduction. Since sex, reproduction, and family relations are no longer necessary, gender hierarchy can also be abolished. Women, as the spiritual peers of men, can participate equally in church leadership.[33]

These two Christologies appear to be opposites. But they were both based on a common presupposition: that patriarchy is the order of creation. They assumed that patriarchy could only be left behind by leaving behind the created order. The equality of men and women "in Christ" was understood as a historical, and not just an eschatological possibility, only when this fusion of patriarchy and creation was uncoupled.

Christology can be liberated

To change this pattern, creation itself must be defined as egalitarian in its authentic nature. This original egalitarianism must be seen, not as a heavenly state before embodiment, but as our original nature as embodied, historical persons. Only then can patriarchy be placed under judgment as an unjust distortion of our human capacities and the social order in our relationships. Equality between men and women can then be envisioned as a social reform within history that restores our original nature, rather than something possible only by an a-historical departure from history and embodied existence.

The basis of this egalitarian anthropology was laid in Europe and America in the late eighteenth and nineteenth centuries. The feudal churches, which reflected the old class hierarchies, were repudiated as representatives of a moribund and unjust society. The redemptive future was severed from its institutionalization in the churches and secularized in reform and revolutionary social movements. These revolutionary liberal and socialist movements rooted themselves in a revised myth of original nature as one of equality of all humans in their "essential" nature. The feudal hierarchy of separate estates was rejected for one of equal political rights.

However, the first stage of such liberal, democratic revolutions only dismantled the hierarchy of aristocracy over the third estate or the bourgeois. It left intact the patriarchal dominance of the male head of family over women, children, propertyless servants, and slaves.[34] The "self-evident" truth that "all men [humans] are created equal and endowed with inalienable rights" would only be gradually applied to these subjugated groups; to propertyless men (universal manhood suffrage); to slaves (abolitionism); and to women (feminism). Socialism would try to extend egalitarianism to economic rights, creating a conflict between political visions of liberty and economic visions of justice that is still unresolved in the late twentieth century.

Yet, by the mid-twentieth century, both liberals and socialists have come to take egalitarian anthropology for granted, in theory. The notion that women are fully human and should have equal rights is officially accepted in both views, however much it may be contradicted in practice. Even the Pope and the Catholic bishops now feel compelled to affirm that women are fully human, are not inferior or defective in human capacities, and are equal sharers in the image of God. But they still cling to a Christology based on a patriarchal anthropology, and attempt to use this in order to exclude women from equality of leadership in the church, while abandoning the more basic exclusion of women from political rights in secular society.[35]

This contradiction between egalitarian anthropology

for secular society, and patriarchal Christology for the church hierarchy reflects a new church-world split. Patriarchy, no longer defensible for secular society, is sacralized as a special sacred order for the church. The result is that Christology loses its basic integration with creation. Christ does not restore and redeem creation, but stands now for a sacred patriarchal order of the church, unconnected with creation. This new creation-redemption split reverses the dilemma of classical Christianity. Creation was assumed to be patriarchal, while redemption in Christ overcame female inferiority, at least spiritually.

In order to recover the integration of Christ and creation essential to a coherent theology, Christology must be recast by integrating it with egalitarian anthropology. Once we have discarded patriarchal anthropology, with its false biological underpinnings that regard women as less complete expressions of human nature than men, we must also affirm women as equally theomorphic. If women share equally in the image of God, then they also share equally in the care of creation. This cannot be limited to a dependent, domestic sphere.

If women are equally theomorphic, then God must be imaged as female as well as male, as the ground of that fullness of personhood present in both women and men. This means that the maleness of the historical Jesus has nothing to do with manifesting a divine "Son" of a divine "Father." Both the gender and the parent-child character of these symbols must be deliteralized. God transcendent is the depth of being which we encounter in redemptive experiences, but as one and the same God.

The problem of Jesus—a male

In Jesus we encounter, paradigmatically, the *Logos-Sophia* of that one God who is both mother and father, liberator, lover, and friend. But how do Christians then deal with the maleness of the historical Jesus, if this no longer is seen as ontologically necessary to manifest a male immanence of a male God? Doesn't the very fact that Jesus is a male continue the assumption that women receive redemption from men, but cannot represent God as redemptive actors?

Christian feminists cannot resolve this problem by suggesting that because Jesus was non-patriarchal in his sensitivity to women and in his vulnerability in suffering, somehow this makes him "feminine," and thus inclusive of women. All this does is make Jesus a model for an androgynous male. But this does nothing to affirm a like holistic humanity for women. Rather, Christians must affirm the particularity of Jesus, not only in gender, but also in ethnicity and in culture. At the same time, we must acknowledge the limitations of any single individual to be universally paradigmatic.

What we find in classical Christology is a dissolution of all other aspects of Jesus' historical particularity, his Jewishness and his first century cultural setting. Yet the symbols elevate his gender to universal ontological significance. Instead, we should encounter Jesus, not only as male, but in all his particularity as a first century Galilean Jew. We then must ask how we can see him as paradigmatic of universal human redemption in a way that can apply to female as well as to male and to people of all ethnicities and all cultures.

This investigation must take us through several stages of revisionist thought about Christology. First we must see that what is paradigmatic about Jesus is not his biological ontology, but rather his person as a lived message and practice. That message is good news to the poor, a confrontation with systems of religion and society that incarnate oppressive privilege, and an affirmation of the despised as loved and liberated by God. Jesus did not just speak this message. He risked his life to embody this presence of God and was crucified by those in power who rejected this message.

Secondly, we must cease to isolate the work of Christ from the ongoing Christian community. This Jesus as a historical figure exemplifies a way of life that is critical in a world where false and oppressive privilege still reign and are still sacralized by religion. As Christians, we are followers of this way. While Jesus is the foundational representative of this way of the cross and liberation, he is not its exclusive possibility. Each Christian must take up this same way, and in so doing, become "other Christs" to one another. The church becomes redemptive community, not by passively receiving a redemption "won" by Christ alone, but rather by collectively embodying this path of liberation in a way that transforms people and social systems.

If we are clear that the redemption signified by Christ is both carried on and communicated through redemptive community, Christ can take on the face of every person and group and their diverse liberation struggles. We must be able to encounter Christ as black, as Asian, as Aboriginal, as women. The coming Christ, then, the uncompleted future of redemption, is not the historical Jesus returned, but rather the fullness of all this human diversity gathered together in redemptive community. This is the "Human One" who is to come, who bears the face of all suffering creatures longing for liberation.

Finally, this way of Christ need not, and should not, be seen as excluding other ways. The creating, inspiriting, and liberating presence of God is present to all humans in all times and places. It has been expressed in many religious cultures, some of which parallel the Christ-way, and some of which complement it with other spiritualities—spiritualities of contemplation for example, or of renewal of nature. The challenge of Christology today may not be to try to extend the Christ symbol to every possible spirituality and culture, but rather to accept its limits. Then we can allow other ways and peoples to flourish in dialogues that can reveal God's many words to us.

Notes

1. This argument that women cannot be ordained because they don't image Christ is found in the "Vatican Declaration on the Question of the Admission of Women to the Ministerial Priesthood," sec. 27 (1976). The argument was repeated in the pastoral letter by Pope John Paul II, "The Dignity and Vocation of Women," sec. 26 (Sept. 31, 1988); and in the pastoral on women by the American Catholic bishops, "One in Christ: A Pastoral Response to the Concerns of Women for Church and Society" (Second Draft), sec. 115, *Origins* (April 5, 1990), 730.

2. For the development of *Logos* Christology in the New Testament, especially in the Gospel of John, see C.H. Dodd, *The Interpretation of the Fourth Gospel* (New York: Cambridge U.P., 1963), 263-285. For its development in the second century, see Erwin Goodenough, *The Theology of Justin Martyr* (Amsterdam: Philo Press, 1968), 139-175.

3. For a critical exegesis of this passage, see Phyllis Bird, "Male and Female He Created Them: Gen. 1:27b in the Context of the Priestly Account of Creation," *Harvard Theological Review* 74:2(1981), 129-175.

4. For essays on the historical development of the exclusion and gradual inclusion of women as imago Dei, see Kari Borresen, ed. *Image of God and Gender Models* (Oslo: Solum Forlag, 1990).

5. Gregory of Nyssa, *De Opif Hom.* 16.7; see Rosemary R. Ruether, "Misogynism and Virginal Feminism in the Fathers of the Church," in R. Ruether, ed. *Religion and Sexism: Images of Women in the Jewish and Christian Traditions* (New York: Simon and Schuster, 1974), 153-155.

6. Augustine, *De Trinitate* 7.7.10.

7. Aristotle, *Gen. An.*, 729b, 737-738.

8. Thomas Aquinas, *Summa Theologica,* pt. 1, q. 92, art. 1.

9. Mary Jane Sherfey, *The Nature and Evolution of Female Sexuality* (New York: Random House, 1972).

10. For example, see Isaiah 42:13-14 and 49:14-15. Also Leonard Swidler, *Biblical Affirmations of Women* (Philadelphia: Westminster Press, 1979), 21-50.

11. See Wisdom of Solomon 6-8.

12. Luke 11:49 and Matthew 11:18-19; see James M. Robinson, "Jesus as Sophos and Sophia: Wisdom Tradition in the Gospels"; and Elisabeth S. Fiorenza, "Wisdom Mythology and the Christological Hymns of the New Testament," in Robert L. Wilkin, ed., *Aspects of Wisdom in Judaism and Early Christianity* (South Bend, IN: Notre Dame Press, 1975), 35ff.

13. See Sigmund Mowinckel, *He That Cometh: The Messiah Concept in the Old Testament and Later Judaism* (Nashville, TN: Abingdon Press, 1955).

14. See Inclusive Language Lectionary Committee, "Son of Man," in *An Inclusive Language Lectionary: Readings for Year A* (Philadelphia: Westminster Press, 1983), appendix.

15. Luke 1:45-55; see Jane Schaberg, *The Illegitimacy of Jesus* (San Francisco, CA: Harper and Row, 1987), 92-107, for the view that Luke believed Mary's son to be illegitimate, and framed the *Magnificat* as a statement that God vindicates the most despised of society, the "fallen" woman.

16. In the synoptic gospels, it is Mary Magdalene who is central to the group of female disciples who are "last at the cross and first at the tomb." Although John puts Mary, Jesus' mother and the disciple John as central figures at the cross, he has the most extended narrative of Mary Magdalene's key role as first witness of the Resurrection. Mary Magdalene plays the key role in gnostic claims for women's apostolic authority. See "The Gospel of Mary," in *The Nag Hammadi Library in English,* ed. John Robinson et al. (San Francisco, CA: Harper and Row, 1977), 471-474.

17. See Edward Schillebeeckx, Jesus: *An Experiment in Christology* (New York: Seabury, 1979), 703, n. 31-33.

18. Joel 2:28-32; Acts 2:17-21.

19. Elisabeth S. Fiorenza, "Word, Spirit and Power: Women in Early Christian Communities," in *Women of Spirit: Female Leadership in the Jewish and Christian Traditions,* ed. R. Ruether (New York: Simon and Schuster, 1979), 39-44.

20. *Didache* 11:3-13:7.

21. Elisabeth S. Fiorenza, *In Memory of Her: A Feminist Theological Reconstruction of Christian Origins* (New York: Crossroad, 1983).

22. The alternative Pauline tradition that sees woman as liberated from marriage into itinerant ministry through chastity is expressed in the non-canonical "Acts of Paul and Thecla." For interpretations of this conflict between eschatological and patriarchal Paulinisms, see Dennis R. MacDonald, *The Legend and the Apostle: The Battle for Paul in Story and Canon* (Philadelphia: Westminster, 1983).

23. I Timothy 2:11-15.

24. Montanist women prophets were accused of abandoning their husbands, which suggests they shared the view of the Acts of Paul and Thecla that women converts to Christ transcended their marital obligations. Gnostics believed that spiritual rebirth enabled women and men to transcend sex and procreation and enter a state of spiritual androgyny. Both groups supported women in ministry. See n. 19 above, Fiorenza, "Word, Spirit and Power," 42; and Elaine Pagels, *The Gnostic Gospels* (New York: Random House, 1979), 48-69.

25. The Council of Elvira, 400 A.D., was the first to mandate clerical continence. The council documents show the connection between clerical sexual continence and obsession with control over female sexuality. See Samuel Laeuchli, *Power and Sexuality: The Emergence of Canon Law at the Council of Elvira* (Philadelphia: Temple U.P., 1982).

26. Fourth century advocates of asceticism, such as Jerome and Athanasius, affirmed three levels of blessing on female states of life: one hundred-fold for virginity, sixty-fold for continent

widowhood, and only thirty-fold for marriage. See William Phipps, *Was Jesus Married?* (New York: Harper and Row, 1970), 142-175.

27. See Susan Wemple, *Women in Frankish Society: Marriage and the Cloister, 500-900 A.D.* (Philadelphia: Pennsylvania U.P., 1983).

28. The period between 500-1500 A.D. saw the continuous struggle of celibate women to retain autonomy and ministry, as well as the resistance of the lower clergy to the imposition of clerical celibacy. See Lina Eckerstein, *Women Under Monasticism* (1898); see John Boswell, *Christianity, Social Tolerance and Homosexuality* (Chicago: Chicago U.P., 1980), for the eleventh century movement to enforce clerical celibacy, seen by the married clergy as a monastic, homosexual movement.

29. There was some notable resistance to Protestant closing of monasteries by nuns. See Jane Douglass, "Women and the Continental Reformation," in *Religion and Sexism,* ed. R. Ruether, 309-314, see n. 5 above.

30. The Puritan leaders placed major emphasis on the household for defining marriage: see William Perkins, *Christian Oeconomie* (London: 1590); and William Gouge, *Of Domestical Duties* (London: 1622).

31. See Joyce L. Erwin, *Womanhood in Radical Protestantism, 1525-1675* (New York: Edwin Mellen Press, 1979), 179ff; also Rosemary Ruether, "Women in Utopian Movements," in R. Ruether and R. Keller, *Women and Religion in America: The Nineteenth Century* (New York: Harper and Row, 1981), 46-100.

32. Eusebius, *Oration on Constantine,* 10.7.

33. The nineteenth century Shakers most fully develop this sexual egalitarianism of the mystical-millennialist tradition. See their bible, *The Testimony of Christ's Second Appearing* (United Society, 1856).

34. The reply of John Adams to his wife's exhortation to "remember the Ladies" in the civil rights of the American Constitution clearly reveals the exclusion, not only of women, but also of slaves, Indians, and propertyless white servants from Adams' concept of those persons with civil rights. See Miriam

Schneir, ed., *Feminism: Essential Historical Writings* (New York: Vintage, 1972), 3-4.

35. This claim to affirm women's secular equality through the concept of *imago Dei* is found in both the pastoral letter on women by John Paul II, and in the American Catholic bishops' draft letter on women; see n. 1 above.

Losing Your Innocence
But Not Your Hope

RITA NAKASHIMA BROCK

Preface

"Who do you say that I am?" This has been one of the most divisive questions in Christendom, even as the church has claimed that it is Jesus Christ who unites the church. In fact, Christological doctrines have only succeeded in uniting those who agree with particular formulations mandated by church authorities. Those formulations, which have shaped the parameters of Christian orthodoxy for years, were developed by only a small segment of people who identified themselves as Christians. Their reality structures, what we might call frameworks of meaning, have determined theological definitions of what is ultimate, what is good, what is evil, and what is life-giving power.

For most of Christian history, church theologians adopted a primary framework of meaning based in patriarchal militarism. Symbols and images for God were male; having power meant dominance, control and the ability to command; and the highest values were loyalty and obedience to authority. In their articulations of abstract, alienating ideas through which they sought to free themselves from the pull of life in this world, they created a perpetual and acute tension between a pure, idealized life with God and the realities of concrete existence, a tension that generated a need for salvation, which they defined in terms of their ideologies of God.[1]

We have in Christology the legacy of those who saw power in hierarchical authority, who believed obedience to the church was the key to ethical behavior, who experienced loving themselves as sinful, who struggled to control, rather than understand, their bodies, who saw love in self-sacrifice and self-denial rather than in intimacy and mutuality, and who decided the salvation granted by God meant the rejection of the flesh and the physical world. That these theologians lived in contexts that encouraged such views means that their theologies are no more or less socially and politically determined than any of ours and that they are no more or less to blame for what they believed. However, I believe we have had enough of that legacy. It is killing us.

In placing such high moral value on obedience to authority, the church advised victims to be self-sacrificing, to forgive their oppressors and be reconciled to them, endangering millions of lives and crippling souls. The church used slavery and servanthood as positive theological paradigms and devalued all things physical, including the earth and its resources. In this century, increasingly, questions of justice and the rejection of an exclusively other-worldly salvation have dominated theology. Material reality—food, education, shelter, politics—have surfaced as theological concerns. But in the subterranean depths of the modern era lurk still the dualistic demons of patriarchy, as feminist analyses of twentieth century theology demonstrate. We need new paradigms and new theologies to guide our faith and our action if we are to survive.

The early Christian witnesses to the church's most important historical encounters with God reflects the patriarchal age in which it was born; yet I believe the life-giving power of those witnesses lies in the tensions that cut against a patriarchal view of the world. There is a small, but constant pull toward mutuality and egalitarianism, a pull suspicious of the individualistic worship of heroes, away from dualism, and against unilateral dominating powers. Evidence from early Christian history—evidence usually ignored—indicates much heterogeneity of belief, the presence of influential women, and the affirmation of pacifism.[2] What I will articulate today in my lecture is not a full blown Christology, based in those less obvious, but key, biblical and historical notes of antipatriarchal pacifism. There is not time for that, and I have done a great deal of that in my book.[3] Instead, I will discuss a shift in theological paradigms that may help us to return to the story of the Jesus movement looking for a new message of hope. I am suggesting the following paradigms based in my experiences of feminist work on child abuse and my struggles to live in this racist society as a mixed-race Asian American woman.

Introduction

At the beginning to the last section of Amy Tan's *The Joy Luck Club,* a mythical dialogue takes place between a baby and grandmother. The dialogue comes after the novel has depicted the intense and painful struggle of Chinese American first generation mothers and their second generation daughters to find lives, to shape meaningful identities, and to understand each other. The dialogue occurs just before the stories of the mothers and daughters coalesce, as the struggle and pain of the mothers begins to empower the daughters. The grandmother says:

> I threw away my foolish innocence to protect myself. And then I taught my daughter, your

mother, to shed her innocence so she would not
be hurt as well.... Then you must teach my
daughter the same lesson. How to lose your
innocence but not your hope. How to laugh forever.[4]

What would happen if we took as a starting point for
our Christological reflections the struggles of mothers to
keep their children alive, to protect them from harm, and
to pass on their knowledge and wisdom to their grandchil-
dren? As far as we know, no one who dominated the theologies of most of Christian history was someone who had
birthed life hot, small, and squirming from between her
own limbs, or someone who had nurtured her pregnant
body for months only to lose the life cherished inside.
Would our understandings of love be different if written
by someone who had known regular physical intimacy and
slept next to her beloved for forty years, or someone who
had felt the daily terror of her spouse's violent outbursts
and borne the wounds of his rage on her body? Would we
understand power differently if we took as our model
someone who had reflected consciously on the conflicts of
having to nurture and empower people dependent on her
while struggling to create something of her own genius, or
who had gone to sleep in terror every night as a child
because the father or brother who was supposed to love
and protect molested instead? Would we think of salvation
in a new way if we listened to someone who had fought to
keep a life and family together under the yoke of slavery,
or someone who used her power to protect her child from
harm while fostering a willfulness that created a human
being independent of her will, a being who could survive
the harsh realities of a government that covertly slaugh-
tered thousands of citizens? How would we think of flesh if
we had the legacy of a woman who developed an acute

atunement to the rhythms of her body, to its physical and emotional messages, in order to nurse a child at her own breast, or one who had struggled day and night for weeks to keep a sick child alive, or someone who had spent years caring for another who could not take care of her or his own physical needs? Can our theology help us laugh forever?

We must, as Jacquelyn Grant argues, pay attention to the "you" in that question "who do you say that I am?"[5] Our answer to the *you* part of the Christological question must be honestly and clearly articulated. At the same time, because of the nature of oppression and politics in our post-Columbus world, we cannot assume all perspectives are equally valid. A theology that marginalizes, makes invisible, or oppresses a particular group of people must be challenged.

While I would not expect the reflections I present below to be universally applicable, they are based in intense reflection on the questions raised by Christology in the context of my struggle to remain an Asian American feminist in the Christian church. I believe that what I offer is better—more life giving, more true to the gospel—than what we have inherited from the dominant, patriarchal tradition. And I welcome the changes in theological conversations possible as an increasing number of persons marginalized or silenced by the church have entered the discussion to answer the Christological question. As part of that discussion, I will explain two important experiences that have shaped my answer to the "you" part of the Christological question. The experiences have had a profound impact on my reflections on the meaning of innocence and obedience in Christological discussions. I will subsequently present a Christological formulation that moves beyond paradigms of innocence and obedience.

The problem with obedience and innocence

As a seminary student in 1974, I participated in a multi-racial summer camp youth education project with about thirty diverse adult staff and 150 high schoolers from Southern California school districts, a human relations project sponsored by the National Conference of Christians and Jews. Subsequently, nearly every summer for a dozen years, I returned for an intense week in which the participants confronted some of the worst evils in our society—racism, sexism, rape, homophobia, gang violence, poverty, drugs, child abuse, and incest—evils endured by society's most defenseless members, its children.[6] I was transformed by my years in that program, a transformation that continually distanced me from the theology I studied in seminary and graduate school.

Slowly, like the rising of the summer sun in a far northern place, levels of insight into pain emerged for me. I grew to understand how the most seemingly carefree persons live in almost daily terror in their own homes. I was forced to understand how the apparently innocent know sexual violation and a profound evil inflicted by those who are supposed to love them, and how the scars of self-hate, fear, and internalized oppression are deeply carved in those who suffer as targets of systems of control and hatred. I felt how paternalistic forms of power immobilize and disempower those struggling against evil, and how relatively few people have been loved and protected enough to thrive and live joyously. The institutions of our culture designed to help youth fail them miserably. I came to know how easily pain becomes hatred of others, ruthless ambition, passive acquiescence, or inconsolable despair when there is no one to heal that pain. While I worked mostly with Asian, female, and mixed parentage youth, I saw this level of suffering in every group, in African,

Hispanic, and European Americans, in males, in gang members, in heterosexuals, gays, and lesbians, and in adult staff, as well as in youth. Through the examples and mutual support of other adult staff, I also gained help to confront my own brokenness and need for power and to realize the harm I could cause.

We did not all suffer in the same ways or for the same reasons, but the level of human brokenness and evil that I witnessed in average, everyday people forced me to rethink theologically everything I had learned about divine power and the meaning of salvation. I was called on often to be the Protestant Chaplain in the program, and I found that the very same religious systems and ideas functioned sometimes to comfort and console and sometimes to disempower and aggravate pain.

I will never forget the night I returned to the staff cabin exhausted and ready for some sleep. A fierce and passionate African American woman whom I greatly admired and who was one of our strongest female staff members had the bunk below me. She was weeping and asked if we could talk. She had just learned that her beloved brother, a youth rehabilitation worker in Detroit, had been murdered on the street. He was the last brother she had alive. She asked me why God took him. She wanted to know why a powerful God did not protect him and the good work he had been doing. The injustice of her brother's death was intensified by her belief in a powerful God who did nothing except to cause her pain. She felt as if she had no strength left and wanted to give up in despair. We held each other, cried, and talked till nearly dawn.

Christian piety, based in traditional theological concepts, a piety my friend had learned, caused her intense pain. To others the same ideas sometimes gave comfort. However, the traditional piety does not empower change.

For it begins by protecting the power of God, power that makes human persons passive recipients of either punishment or grace. What my theological training had not given me was the ability to acknowledge my own pain and take responsibility for healing it, and it did not give me a way to empower those in pain to deal with the people and systems destroying them. I turned for resources, in those moments, to what had empowered me, which were social and political movements—Civil Rights, Peace Groups, and Feminism. At the same time, my work with that summer program also forced me to rethink the polarized and self-righteous dichotomies of oppressor and oppressed that I learned in those activist movements, even as my commitments to the political transformation of American society and the world were deepened.

What I saw in the privatized world of Protestant Christianity was the isolation of individuals into solitary worlds of suffering, especially when the violation they experienced touched most deeply into the psyche and body. Even those who did not blame themselves for their own pain, who knew that they did not deserve what happened to them, felt embarrassed about being victims, about being violated persons.

The Christian use of father-child images for divine-human relationships mystifies abuse. Rather than being taught to respect their own bodies, their own feelings, their own rights to be loved and valued, children are taught to obey authority, especially fathers and priests, two groups that sometimes abuse them. Children are taught to allow themselves to be controlled by the superior will of authority, as Jesus was subject to the will of his Father, rather than to trust their own feelings first. They are taught adults are always right, and that if a child is disobedient, abuse is deserved. Children are, in their pain, often isolated by fear and guilt as they struggle to love those who hurt them. Theologically, we are told that the Father God, who can do no wrong, sent his own Son to be killed and the good, obedient Son went willingly, without complaint. If cosmic child abuse, to save humanity, is acceptable, and human parents are to obey the example set by the Father God, then the violation of children can be justified on the same grounds.[7] Protection from such abuse—a false protection—comes from being obedient and innocent.

Such obedience and innocence are, of course, no protection at all. For example, Sheila Redmond in an essay "Christian Virtues and Child Sexual Abuse" points out that Maria Goretti is held up as a model to Catholic Christians because she chose to be hacked to death rather than be sullied sexually.[8]

> She wasn't "spoiled goods," something that the doctors checked out at the hospital immediately so that they could reassure her mother that the worst had not happened to her...If you were assaulted as a child and you did not fight off the attacker to death, you must be guilty of some sin, some inherent weakness; it must be your fault.[9]

One of the messages of this story is that it is better to die pure than to survive. To be violated is to be guilty. For purity, that state of innocence in which one is without guilt because one has not experienced or known evil or sin, is better than possessing the strength and wits to survive, to have faced evil squarely, borne its terrors, and lived.

The isolation of guilt and fear is one thing that distinguishes the abuse of children from the oppression of groups of adults. Isolation silences and kills, and often involves amnesia about abuse. Oppression is the forceful subordination of a group of people by a system for the purposes of those who benefit from the oppression.

Liberation from oppression lies in a group's subjective awareness of the wrong done to them and a conscious striving to overcome oppression. The two terms oppression and liberation are inadequate to address the situation of children in families, for abusive families do not teach children a critical collective consciousness about being abused. Neither children nor women automatically have available to them any sort of collective group consciousness about oppression. Such consciousness emerges because oppressed groups are often put together and separated from their oppressors, a separation from which a critical consciousness can be born.[10] Both children and women live with, often love, and even sleep with, those who hurt them. They sustain relationships of paternalistic exchange with those who cause them pain. In striving to be good and obedient, they may feel some sense of false control over their suffering. For the sake of protection and physical affection, a child may endure sexual abuse and then feel as if her or his own needs and behaviors caused the abuse. For the sake of financial support or race or class privilege, a woman may stay with her abusive husband. Children and women often experience themselves as both victims and agents and remain silent about their suffering. They can belong to both oppressed and oppressor groups while experiencing unspeakable suffering. In belonging to an oppressed group, they may have a sophisticated understanding of the politics of oppression and a powerful history of activism for liberation while at the same time living silently with crippling abuse. I believe the theological work being done in liberationist forms of theology is crucial for Christian faith, but my own work has been mainly concerned with creating new theological paradigms and images that empower persons to acknowledge and heal from suffering caused by our most intimate relationships so that we might be healed for the work of love and justice.[11]

My experiences as a mixed-race Asian American woman have also moved me away from theological paradigms of obedience and innocence, as I have struggled to survive life in the dominant culture of the United States. For many Asian American women, the feminist religious and theological communities have not been hospitable places, partly because our perspectives are sorely lacking.[12] Many Asian American women articulate approaches to political and theological questions different from those offered by most Western feminists. Because Western thinking, including feminist thinking, tends to be either/or, there is little recognition that in taking an opposing stand, one often appropriates the methods and metaphysical assumptions of one's opponents because one shares cultural similarities including language structures and modes of rhetoric with one's opponents.

The tendency to think polemically, especially with regard to political issues, such as oppression, is less characteristic of Asian Americans, partly because of Asian patterns of thinking and partly because Asian Americans do not always develop a critical consciousness of oppression. Asian thinking, found especially in first generation Asian Americans, is often paradoxical, embracing a both/and approach to oppositions and intuitive and holistic modes of apprehension. This thinking recognizes that dualisms require each other and are artificially constructed as oppositions. Today, nisei and sansei Asian Americans do not always live in Asian American communities and do not have access to a group critical consciousness of racism and oppression. Instead, we cope with such issues by denial or by silent and lonely suffering, suffering analogous to abuse, rather than to oppression.[13]

Navigating through paradoxical, ambiguous territory

is a major element in the works of Asian American women, writings which describe our search for identity in complex environments. This maneuvering within ambiguity is guided by a respect for wisdom that rejects damaging demands to be obedient and innocent. In works by writers such as Cynthia Kadohato, Maxine Hong Kingston, Wendy Law-Yone, and Amy Tan the central female characters are skeptical about authority and refuse to be innocent.[14] They struggle to understand the sources of their pain; they do what they must to survive, and they remember everything, holding on to all the parts of their lives no matter how troubling. For example, in the Kadohato novel, *The Floating World*, the adolescent narrator refuses to assist her dying grandmother because the woman has tormented her and she chooses consciously to live with the guilt of letting her die alone.

Perhaps because the cultural roots of Asian American identity lie to some extent in Confucian values, which respect the wisdom and sophistication of age, rather than the innocence associated with children, innocence is placed in these Asian American women's novel in proper perspective. The writers depict innocence as something we must outgrow, or else we risk remaining superfluous and disempowered, which is the designated state of women and children. Innocence may be appropriate to babies, but innocence in adults is dangerous. Innocence is not a survival skill. It neither nurtures and empowers life nor passes it on. Cunning, quick wits, a tolerance for ambiguity, skills at manipulation, a creative imagination, sound moral reflection, and an active sense of agency emerge with the rejection of innocence.

In many of the works by Asian American women, knowing who we are involves a struggle with forces that threaten to separate us from our histories. But remembering those histories includes an assiduous avoidance of nostalgia for the past, for a longing for a return to tradition. Memory is a source of self-awareness and survival, but it is careful, demystifying the oppressive authority of tradition because this memory occurs in a new context that allows more dislocation from tradition. Little is forgotten; even the painful and problematic are remembered, but we struggle to be neither nostalgic about our experiences nor self-hating. The past is embraced critically.

The above writers speak of the complex forces of war and oppression that required them, or their ancestors, to cast their lots with marginalized and suffering people in a hostile new land. They refuse to blame others or to justify self-righteously the actions of Asian American women, even as they acknowledge piercing angers about the pain of racism, poverty, and misogyny. In a fragmented, confusing, and deconstructed world, they struggle to reconstruct meaning. They reject any intellectual apartheid that forces either/or choices and they reject a cynical fragmentation into total relativism.[15]

Rather than seeking to be good or clinging to trust in the power of others, which is how one remains innocent, the stories of Asian American women depict them as seeking to minimize the forces that threaten their lives and those they love. They reject innocence in order to enlarge and enhance their capacities to alleviate pain and sustain the loving bonds that keep people alive. They are neither innocent nor obedient; they learn to be strong, strategically smart, skeptical, cunning, caring, and wise.

This rejection of obedience and innocence is in sharp contrast to Western Christian attitudes that prize them, even in adults. Doctrines about the sinless purity of Jesus and the image of him as an innocent lamb taken obediently to slaughter reinforce the idea that victims ought to be innocent and virtuous or else pain and suffering are deserved, even though the gospels tend to depict a more ambiguous and politically savvy Jesus. If we romanticize victims and want innocence, do we not say that suffering is deserved by the guilty and the knowledgeable, that mechanisms of oppression are not inherently wrong, but serve the protection of goodness, and that punishing the wicked is a divine mandate, no matter what structures do this because obedience is the way to avoid punishment. An emphasis on the innocence of victims can lead both to the tendency to blame victims, if anything can be found wrong with them or if they disobey their oppressors, and to dichotomies that paint oppressors as one-dimensionally evil and victims as helpless.

The structure of Christian theological thinking, and even of English itself, reinforces dichotomous dualisms of oppressor and oppressed. We are asked to identify as one or the other, but what if we are both? Most of us are both and we are more than both. We live in complex relationships of power in which the abuse of other human beings and our environment are part of our potential, even as we are vulnerable to the abuse of others. But we have no language beyond black or white, up or down, and above or below to talk about the politics of our lives; and so our theology talks about the oppressed being lifted up, about reversals of power, about exaltation and humiliation.

Life in the messy middle

Sara Ruddick in her book *Maternal Thinking* discusses the ethics of being in the middle, of the ethical thinking involved when women live in oppressive circumstances and possess life and death power over the lives of children. She tells the story of a young mother named Julie Olsen Edwards, whose first child was an extremely difficult, colicky baby.[16] Julie lived in a third-floor apartment, and her husband was often away studying and working. For ten months, she never slept more than two hours at one time and lived with intense sleep deprivation caring for her sick child without the financial resources to hire help. One night, as she lay sleeping, Julie heard the baby's screams and she said:

> You toss your body back and forth, arch your back and wail and call. Trembling, I...try to speak, to soothe...but my throat constricts in silent screaming and I find I cannot touch your tangled blankets.... I picture myself lifting your tininess in both my hands and flinging you at the window. Mixed with my choking I can almost hear the glass as it would smash and I see your body, your perfect body, swirl though the air and land three stories below on the pavement.

Sickened by her vision, Julie vomits, changes the baby's diaper, gives her a bottle and barricades the closed door so she cannot be with her child. Later the same night, because she wants both to kill and to nurture her child, she wraps it up and carries it, riding on the bus all night, thinking the child would be safe with her if they were not alone.

Here are anger and pain mixed with love and fear, helplessness and hopelessness mixed with decisions to act and a desire to keep going. This is life in the messy middle of things, where our circumstances, our loves, our fears, and our commitments enmesh us daily in ambiguous choices as we struggle to resist evil both within us and outside us. In her intensely willful decision to use her power to save her child from herself, Julie is more than oppressor or oppressed. She is an agent of salvation.

This messy middle is explored by Nel Noddings in her work on a phenomenology of evil, *Women and Evil*.[17] She begins by deconstructing innocence. Noddings argues that a woman's moral claim on life has been understood to rest in her feminine nature, an ideology of the feminine soul developed in the nineteenth century.[18] A woman's unconscious essence has been associated with an archetypal chaste goodness. A woman's moral achievements are not understood as acts of her will.[19] Her decisions are not seen as carefully considered and arrived at through thought. Rather, a woman's goodness is seen as evidence of a superior force working through her, which is associated with her biological destiny as wife and mother. In Christianity, this force is God. This is not her destiny to choose, but one given her. Hence, her goodness is innocent—unconscious and passive.

Similarly, children are considered good because they obey the will of a superior parental force which works on them to create moral goodness. The association of women with innocence may also explain why women are so often depicted as childlike, not only in the West but also in many Asian countries. The presence of male dominance is associated in Asia and the West with this kind of essentialist thinking about gender and with the passive infantilization of women, such that cultural practices and attitudes enforce the helplessness of women. In the face of evil, an innocent woman must protect her innocence and become a victim. To protest, to fight back, is to assert too much will and to lose her claim to protection.

Man, according to Noddings, is traditionally understood to be the intellectual agent of morality, who uses his will, like God, to make ethical decisions. His realm is the public sphere in which "real" ethical choices are made. If a woman claims that she makes ethical choices, this claim makes her like a man and puts her in a foreign sphere. Since she cannot be a man and has lost her ability to rely on her nature, she is morally unreliable. Willfulness in women is dangerous, is evil. In other words, to be good, a woman must be innocent of active agency and conscious knowledge of her own choices. She must fulfill her role in the domestic sphere, which is the only place of protection for her. The savage irony here is that the domestic sphere is one of high danger for women and children. In constructing another way to understand moral behavior, I suggest we must give up the ideology of obedience and innocence.

As resources for understanding the power of human agency for good, Noddings looks to the activity of women who struggle to alleviate pain, maintain relationships, and empower the actions of others—women who seek to be wise. She argues that life is ambiguous and that evil will never be destroyed or overcome, but it can be managed in such a way as to make life more humane if we struggle to minimize pain, to keep connections to life-giving relationships, and to work against what makes us helpless. She is developing, I would say, an ethics for agents of salvation.

In refusing obedience and innocence and seeing the agency of human action as the tool of minimizing evil, we can view women and children not simply as victims to be pitied or helped, but as agents of our own lives, survivors who are neither innocent nor good, but who, within the limits of power given them, make conscious choices for good and ill. Neither are oppressors simply evil, but they must be made accountable for their behavior and expected to do better. We are all, or at least most of us, both conscious agents *and* victims enmeshed in the same systems of violence and oppression that afflict us all. In fact, I would argue that the loss of innocence and the acceptance of our responsibility for struggling to minimize evil, the knowledge that we have some power, even if only minimal, to contribute to life-giving forces is a knowledge that gives hope. Hence, we must lose our innocence in order to gain hope.

The questions that emerge from a refusal to cling to innocence and to split our identities into externally projected forms of evil and internally defensive forms of self-righteousness are not who is right and who is wrong. Instead I want to ask what strategies can we develop for minimizing harm and what resources can we develop to give dignity and agency to people? How can we speak to each other with mutual respect, so that our speaking is neither accusatory nor acquiescent? How can we identify the problem in ways that allow us all to be agents of salvation, people who can take responsibility? To answer these questions requires not obedience and innocence, but discernment, courage, solidarity, and the affirmation that we live life in the messy middle.

A Christology of discernment, courage, and solidarity

To begin a Christology of discernment, courage, and solidarity, we must, I believe, be willing to stay in the messy middle. As human beings, we are fundamentally relational. We are born neither essentially good and pure nor evil and sinful. We are born with needs for physical care, for respect, and for love and the extent to which our families and communities provide our basic needs determines the extent to which we will have personal resources for caring for, respecting, and loving others. The extent to which our families and communities resist the evils of oppression is the extent to which we will learn resistance. The extent to which we struggle with forces of anger, hate, and destruction within ourselves, and the extent to which our adult lives exhibit compassion, joy, and hope are largely governed by the social and political forces that are around us like the air we breathe. We could not become so evil, build such devastatingly destructive and horrifying systems if we were not so vulnerable to the power of others. And we could not become so caring, so hungry for justice, and so respectful of others' lives if we had not already had glimpses that made us ready for love and justice. Because human life is fundamentally relational, we are never entirely determined by our past histories. The world around us can destroy our lives with a brutality we never knew as children, and that same world offers us grace through our willingness to take responsibility for our personal histories, including facing the pain in our lives.

The spiritual power that undergirds and enables that taking of responsibility is the power of God incarnate, not in the power to demand obedience, but in the power of love which draws us to each other in our hunger for mutuality, in our deepest desires to know another fully, and to be in social relationships that empower creativity, passion, and well-being. Love, when it is divinely inspired, when it is life-giving, lively, creative, and profoundly transformative, is fully mutual, intimate, and nurturing of all involved in it. That power of God as love is what Audre Lorde has called the power of the erotic, the power of our deepest desires.[20]

While Christian theology has claimed that God is love and that justice is crucial to human society, it has continued to use nonrelational, individualistic paradigms to develop ideologies of love and justice in the life of Jesus. For both love and justice to exist, there must be more than one person, no matter how spectacular he may be. For the power of God as love to be fully incarnate, the full presence of God cannot reside in Jesus only, but in the messy middle of our relationships. Love is not a possession, a virtue we possess and parcel out to worthy recipients. Love and justice are events, ongoing processes of synergistic creation born through the wholehearted participation of two or more people gathered in their name.

To live in communities struggling for love and justice requires not obedience, but moral discernment. In the constantly changing realties of communities of struggle, we must remain ever alert, open, and careful because sources of evil may not come simply from an external enemy, but also from within our communities and from within ourselves. We must maintain the courage to stand up to evil, to challenge its infliction of suffering, at the same time we remain suspicious of our most self-righteous polemics and blindly defensive postures. We must cherish our anger at injustice at the same time we are attuned to the opportunities to heal the pain that lies below anger. We must become willful agents of salvation.

If we are to construct a Christology outside the frameworks of obedience and innocence, we must make certain basic and fundamental shifts in interpreting the meaning of Christian origins. A key shift is the assertion that no one's violent, premature, and unjust death is willed by God. All such death, including the crucifixion of Jesus, is tragic and should be mourned as tragic. As long as we continue to say that his death was necessary to save us, we are saying that those who hated, feared, and killed him were right and that those who loved him and wanted him to live were wrong. Hate is not right and love wrong. Jesus did not die to save us. He died because the political, patriarchal powers of his day saw the danger of his life and his movement to their system of oppression.

The power of love incarnate revealed in the Jesus movement is not one of obedience and punishment, but one of mutuality, of the healing of pain, of responsibility for each other, of nurturing care, and of our deepest hungers for justice—of, in their best sense, Jewish covenant and shalom. God does not will things for us, but nurtures us to our own willfulness, to be a thoughtful compassionate discernment. In that willfulness, we become not children or servants of God, but friends. Jesus' willfulness, his radical stubbornness in the face of intimidation and terrorism is evidence of his impassioned commitments to what he loved and his willingness to risk everything for that love. Such willfulness becomes especially important when we live under powers that seek to make us passive and acquiescent.

That Jesus' willfulness led to his death is not what saves us. We are saved by the resurrection community, the saving remnant who watched him die and returned to his grave to care for the body of the one they loved. This saving remnant is not innocent. They have, as Luke tells us, been cured of many demons. They have known and faced the brokenness of their own lives, and in losing their innocence, they have learned willfulness and lived in hope. They are also not innocent because they know they are afraid when they return to Jesus' grave. They are willful because they know the risks they take, and they must overcome their fear in order to keep hope alive. Their fear comes from their lack of innocence, from their knowledge of the potentially fatal consequences of their risks. This resurrection community is ourselves. We are called to be the wise and willful saving remnant that refuses to give up even when we are afraid.

No one else can stop the suffering in our world but our own courage and willingness to act in the midst of the awareness of our own fragility. No one else can die for us. Each death is a tragedy we mourn. Our wise, willful actions carried out in the fragile, resilient relationships of the saving remnant generates the divine power that makes and sustains life. In that power, we find the sacred, life-giving mystery through which we love each other willfully and hopefully in the face of suffering. In that loving, we stand together as witnesses against evil. In that solidarity, we wisely and willfully participate in love and justice. And so, in losing our innocence we gain our hope, and perhaps we can learn to laugh forever.

Notes

1. The creation of a need for salvation in all the so-called "higher" religions, which base themselves in abstract, universalistic ideologies, is discussed by Shmuel Eisenstadt in his essay "The Axial Age: The Emergence of Transcendental Visions and the Rise of Clerics," *European Journal of Sociology* 23, 2(1982): 294-314.

2. See Walter Bauer, *Orthodoxy and Heresy in Earliest Christianity,* ed. Robert Kraft and Gerhard Krodel (Philadelphia: Fortress Press, 1971); Elisabeth Schüssler-Fiorenza, *In Memory of Her: A Feminist Theological Reconstruction of Christian Origins* (New York: Crossroad Press, 1983); and Elaine Pagels, *The Gnostic Gospels* (New York: Random House, 1979).

3. *Journeys by Heart: A Christology of Erotic Power* (New York: Crossroad Press, 1988).

4. Amy Tan, *The Joy Luck Club* (New York: G.P. Putnam's Sons, 1989), 213.

5. In "Subjectification as Requirement for Christological Construction," *Lift Every Voice: Constructing Christian Theologies from the Underside,* ed. Mary Potter Engel and Susan Thistlethwaite (New York: Harper & Row, 1991).

6. A sample of one week's experiences in this program is shown in the 1981 documentary film, "Coming of Age," produced and directed by Dennis Hicks and available through the National Council of Christians and Jews, 635 Harvard Blvd., Los Angeles, CA 90005.

7. Philip Greven poignantly demonstrates this in his book, *Spare the Child: The Religious Roots of Punishment and the Psychological Impact of Physical Abuse* (New York: Alfred A. Knopf, 1991).

8. In *Christianity, Patriarchy, and Abuse: A Feminist Critique,*

ed. Joanne Carlson Brown and Carol R. Bohn (New York: Pilgrim Press, 1989).

9. Brown and Bohn, *Christianity, Patriarchy, and Abuse,* 76.

10. Isolation is related to the dynamic that Gerda Lerner describes in *The Creation of Patriarchy* as the difference between the related terms oppression and liberation (New York: Oxford University Press, 1986), appendix, 231-243. Lerner's analysis is restricted to women, but I believe there are aspects of it that also apply to children.

11. The person that has most influenced my intellectual understanding of intimate abuse is Alice Miller, especially her books, *The Drama of the Gifted Child: How Narcissistic Parents Form and Deform the Emotional Lives of Their Talented Children* (New York: Basic Books, 1981); *For Your Own Good: Hidden Cruelty in Child-Rearing and the Roots of Violence* (New York: Farrar, Straus & Giroux, 1984); and *Thou Shalt Not Be Aware: Society's Betrayal of the Child* (New York: Farrar, Straus & Giroux, 1984).

12. See Rita Nakashima Brock and Naomi Southard, "The Other Half of the Basket: Asian American Women and the Search for a Theological Home," in *The Journal of Feminist Studies in Religion* 3 no. 2(Fall 1987): 135-149.

13. For a poignant depiction of such isolation, see David Mura, *Turning Japanese: Memoirs of a Sansei* (New York: Atlantic Books, 1991).

14. *The Floating World* (New York: Viking Press, 1989); *The Woman Warrior* (New York: Random House, 1975); *The Coffin Tree* (New York: Alfred A. Knopf, 1983), and *The Joy Luck Club* (New York: G.P. Putnam Sons, 1989), respectively.

15. Han Suyin uses the term intellectual apartheid to describe the choices forced on her because she is bi-racial. See Han Suyin, *Between Worlds: Woman Writes of Chinese Ancestry* (New York: Pergamon Press, 1990).

16. Ruddick, *Maternal Thinking: Toward a Politics of Peace* (Boston: Beacon Press, 1989): 65 ff, cites this story from "Motheroath," *Women's Studies Quarterly* 12 no. 2(Summer 1984): 25-28.

17. Nell Noddings, *Women and Evil* (Berkeley, CA: University of California Press, 1989).

18. See Marilyn Chapin Massey, *Feminine Soul: The Fate of an Ideal* (Boston: Beacon Press, 1985).

19. Noddings, *Women and Evil,* see n. 17 above. Noddings' analysis of women's experiences applies most clearly to middle class white women, but the expectations of women she discusses are often applied to all women.

20. Audre Lorde, "Uses of the Erotic: The Erotic as Power," *Sister Outsider: Essays and Speeches* (Trumansburg, NY: The Crossing Press, 1984), 53-59.

"Come to My Help, Lord, For I'm In Trouble": Womanist Jesus and the Mutual Struggle for Liberation

JACQUELYN GRANT

I looked at my hands, to see if I was the same person now that I was free. There was such a glory over everything, the sun came like gold through the trees, and over the fields, and I felt like I was in heaven.

I had crossed the line of which I had so long been dreaming. I was free; but there was no one to welcome me to the land of freedom, I was a stranger in a strange land, and my home after all was down in the old cabin quarter, with the old folks, and my brothers and sisters. But to this solemn resolution I came; I was free, and they should be free also; I would bring them all there. Oh, how I prayed then, lying all alone on the cold, damp ground; "Oh, dear Lord," I said, "I ain't got no friend but you. Come to my help, Lord, for I'm in trouble!"[1]

"I'm in trouble," Harriett Tubman said. What was the source of her trouble? She was finally free. Her prayers had been answered; her dream had come true. She had reached the "state" which she perceived to be like heaven—freedom—the long awaited reality. Freedom in her understanding was the essence of the good news of the gospel! We are taught that the Christian response is to go forth in all the world and "spread the gospel" to others. Even from a Christian point of view, then, it is not difficult to understand the yearnings of Harriet Tubman. The gospel experienced, must be shared; freedom experienced, must be shared. However, it is not uncommon for a gospel encounter to create dilemmas which are not easily resolved. The gospel keeps us in a perpetual cycle of decision making. We must say "yes" to the gospel, and that "yes" is manifested in life as lived daily. Or we say no by our inactivity. The dilemma for Tubman meant trouble. Just as life in general for black people was a perpetual state of "trouble," certainly for an escaped slave the thought of going back into the den of iniquity was a source of grave concern.

For Tubman the challenge was both personal and religious. The will for her family members and others to have the "heaven-like" experience was matched only by her Christian beliefs. The nature of her Christian belief was such that, as sung in the old time gospel song, she "just couldn't keep it to herself." Yes, freedom experienced is indeed freedom shared. What happens when the nature of the gospel and the nature of the existential situation render one in direct conflict with the "human principalities and powers that be"? Isn't that often what being a Christian means—challenging unjust and evil powers?

In the experiences of black women, Jesus was ever-present. He has commonly been perceived and experienced as being present in "times of trouble." Ntozake

Shange commented through one of her characters in her choreopoem, *For Colored Girls Who Have Considered Suicide When the Rainbow is Enuf,* that to speak of black women's existence as "colored and sorry" is to be redundant.[2] Sadness and sorrow (the pain, the sufferings) are perpetually a part of the African American woman's reality; so much so that, whatever else the consideration, these components are always present in the lives of black women. Consequently, to be "colored and sorry" is to be redundant. In the same way, one could say that to speak of black women's existence as being in trouble, or more to the point, having trouble, is to be redundant. The multi-dimensional nature of black women's oppression means that "trouble" is always in the way. Contrary to another old gospel song, "Trouble in My Way, We Have to Hide Sometimes," it is literally impossible to hide. The pervasiveness and interconnectedness of racism, sexism, classism, and other forms of oppression which define a good portion of the lives of black women make "trouble" inescapable. Jesus, for many black women, has been the consistent force which has enabled them not only to survive the troubles of the world, but to move beyond them.

In this essay, I will explore three sources of the troubles of the African American women, with special reference to the problem of Christology. Essentially, I argue that the central Christological problem rests in the fact that Jesus Christ has been and remains imprisoned by the socio-political interests of those who historically have been the keepers of the principalities and powers. This Jesus has been a primary tool for undergirding oppressive structures. I will discuss the troubles of African American women by exploring three ways in which Jesus has been imprisoned:

1) The imprisonment of Jesus Christ by patriarchy;
2) The imprisonment of Jesus Christ by white
   supremacy; and
3) The imprisonment of Jesus Christ by the privileged
   class.

Then, in conclusion, I will explore the implications for the liberation or the redemption of Jesus Christ based on the lived realities of African American women.

The historical imprisonment of Jesus Christ by patriarchy

It is no accident that in the course of Christian history, men have defined Jesus Christ so as to undergird their own privileged positions in the church and society. This is evidenced by the fact that Jesus Christ is used to justify the subordination of women in the church. An understanding of the context in which this kind of interpretation emerges, explains the interpretation itself.

An aspect of the social context in which Christianity, as we know it, developed, and in which we now live, is patriarchy. Defined in the male consciousness, patriarchy assumes male dominance and control making normative the centrality of men and the marginality of women. The primary roles of men and the secondary roles of women effectively insure a hierarchy in sex or gender roles. Moreover, patriarchy embraces "the whole complex of sentiments, the patterns of cognition and behavior, and the assumptions about human nature and the nature of the cosmos that have grown out of a culture in which men have dominated women."[3] Patriarchy is a way of looking at reality so that role assignments are not arbitrarily given; they are a part of the rational and systematic structures of perceived reality itself. Patriarchy has been called a "conceptual trap" which ensnares its victims and keeps them in place through the constant reinforcement of society which cooperates to keep the male status quo in place. It's like being in a room, and unable to imagine anything in the world outside of it.[4] As a result of patriarchy, neither men nor women can imagine themselves outside of their pre-scribed roles. When they do, and when and if action fol-lows, they are treated as "exceptions" as long as the system remains in place. Living within these parameters means living with dualisms which effectively keep men in superi-or and women in inferior positions, thus rendering men as authority figures over women. Just as Jesus has power and authority over men and women, men have power and authority over women and children.

The Christological import of these effects of patri-archy is that the divine is generally associated with what it means to be male in this society. In another place, I have explored the specific correlation between patriarchal assumptions about gender roles and the issue of women's leadership in the church.[5] However, it is enough to say here that the lingering controversies regarding leadership, ordi-nation, and placement of women in the church are over-whelmingly and distortedly Christological.

Women have been denied humanity, personhood, leadership, and equality in the church and in society because of the church's history of negative Christology. This negative Christology has resulted primarily from an over-emphasis on the maleness of Jesus. The maleness, in actuality, has become idolatrous. In fact, the maleness of Jesus has been so central to our understanding of Jesus Christ that even the personality of Jesus and interpreta-tions of Christ have been consistently distorted. In effect, Jesus has been imprisoned by patriarchy's obsession with the supremacy of maleness.

Using gender analysis, many of the historical, biblical and theological interpretations have been challenged by feminist theologians who have worked diligently to overcome the sin of patriarchy. They have been able to break from the conceptual trap by taking seriously women's experiences as a context and a source for biblical interpretation. Seeing reality through the eyes of women has led to a rereading of biblical texts and a consequent revision of biblical and theological interpretations. Some feminists have been able to re-form Jesus; others have attempted to liberate Jesus and women by suggesting that though Jesus can be seen in relation to the male physical reality, Christ transforms maleness and may take on female or feminine forms. Still other feminists have argued the uselessness of these revisionist approaches, for in their views, to speak of Christianity and patriarchy is to be redundant.

As victims of sexism, black women, along with other women, are once removed from the image of God. As I explore the problem of Christology from the perspective of an African American woman, the question of sexism and its function in the historic oppression of women must be adequately addressed. Feminists have provided some significant analyses that have helped in breaking the prison of patriarchy, pointing a direction for eliminating the sin of sexism from our lives, our churches, and our societies.

The historical imprisonment of Jesus by white supremacy ideology

For African American women, however, the question is much broader than the sin of sexism. Racism, in the view of many, has been the basic defining character in the lives of African American women in North America. Recent publications continue to document the contemporary manifestations of racism in our everyday lives. Unfortunately, the church has not escaped this sinful reality. On the contrary, the church has been a bastion of the sin of racism. This is reflected not only in the practice of much of its populace, but in its structures and in its theology. This is nowhere more apparent than in the negative color symbolism institutionalized in Christian theology. The constant battle between light and dark, good and evil (God and devil), white and black, is played out daily in racial politics of the dominant Euro-American culture, and at the same time, theologically legitimated and institutionalized in the racial imageries of the divine. The racism is reflected in the fact that white imagery is presented as normative to the exclusion of any other possible imagery of Jesus or God.

These oppressive ideologies and theologies have been developed in the context of white supremacy. The ideology of white supremacy produces the kind of racism with which we have been afflicted throughout most of the history of this continent. Racism, according to Joel Kovel, "...is the tendency of a society to degrade and do violence to people on the basis of race, and by whatever mediations may exist for this purpose."[6] These mediations are manifested in different forms, and are carried on through various disciplines: psychology, sociology, history, economics, art and symbolism of the dominant group. Racism is the domination of a people which is justified by the dominant group on the basis of racial distinctions. It is not only individual acts, but a collective, institutionalized activity. As C. Eric Lincoln observed:

> [f]or racism to flourish with the vigor it enjoys in America, there must be an extensive climate of acceptance and participation by large numbers of people who constitute its power base. It is the consensus of private persons that gives racism its derivative power.... The power of racism is the

power conceded by those respectable citizens who by their actions or inaction communicate the consensus which directs and empowers the overt bigot to act on their behalf.[7]

Racism, then is not only measurable by individual actions, but by institutional structures, and theoretical precepts. Its presence is guaranteed even in the absence of any particular human carriers.

Christological expressions of this racism are represented in our common images of Jesus Christ and of God. The irrationality used here is similar to that used in the sin of sexism. For example, even though we insist that God is a spirit and Jesus died for us all, we persist in deifying the maleness of both God and Jesus, certainly giving men a social, political and theological edge over women. With regard to the sin of racism, though we claim God as spirit and Jesus as being for all, we have consistently and historically represented God and Jesus as white. We have in fact deified "whiteness." Even the popular culture reflected by Hollywood (cf. the movie *Oh God*) gives us a God who resides in pure whiteness, and is represented by "an old white man." In other words, Christian consensus (albeit based upon and grounded in the history of theology) enables "respectable Christians" to accept without question the destructive negative color symbolism of Christian theology. No wonder some black folks are still singing and praying "Lord, wash me whiter than snow,"[8] despite the problematic nature of related scriptures.

In the white church tradition, Jesus Christ has functioned as a status quo figure. Because historically Christology was constructed in the context of white supremacist ideology and domination, Christ has functioned to legitimate these social and political realities. Essentially, Christ has been white. This is evidenced not only in the theological imagery, but also in the physical imagery of Jesus himself. In a society in which "white is right and black stays back," and white symbolizes good and black, evil, certainly there would be socio-political ramifications of color with respect to Jesus. The implication that white/light is good and black/dark is evil functions, not only with respect to humanity, but also with respect to human's concept of their deity. The late Bishop Joseph Johnson made the point this way:

> Jesus Christ has become for the white church establishment the "white Christ," blue eyes, sharp nose, straight hair, and in the image of the black man's oppressor. The tragedy of this presentation of Jesus Christ by the white church establishment is that he has been too often identified with the repressive and oppressive forces of prevailing society. The teachings of the "white Christ" have been used to justify wars, discrimination, segregation, prejudice, and the exploitation of the poor and the oppressed people of the world. In the name of this "white Christ" the most vicious form of racism has been condoned and supported.[9]

To counteract this historical and theological trend, black theologians have called not only for a new departure in theology but even more specifically for a new Christological interpretation. The white Christ must be eliminated from the black experience and the concept of a black Christ must emerge. Theologians like Cone, Wilmore, Cleage, and others have argued this point from various perspectives. Some argue for literal blackness; some for symbolic blackness. The point is to acknowledge the oppressive ways in which the negative images have functioned for black and white people. It is a question of images in relation to human beings. We have been taught to believe that blacks are not made in the image of God. For this reason many still harbor beliefs, strong feelings, and attitudes about the inferiority of blacks even when our intellects tell us otherwise.

African American women as women and as black persons are thus twice removed from the image of God.

The historical imprisonment of Jesus by the privileged class

For African American women, the issue is broader than sexism and racism. The image of Jesus as servant has consistently been used to reinforce servant bondage among black people. Explorations into the area of domestic servanthood illustrate my point. In particular, a look at the relationship between white women and black women vis-à-vis slavery and domestic service demonstrates that the Christian notion of servanthood has historically been used to reinforce a servant, subservient, and obedient mentality in politically oppressed people. The shorter catechism taught to slaves went like this:

Q: Who made you?
A: God made me.
Q: Why did God make you?
A: To serve my earthly master.[10]

Even after slavery it appears that the attitude survived, for black people in general and black women in particular have always been disproportionately relegated to servant positions. They were given to believe that it was not only their civil duty, but their Christian or heavenly duty to obey. In other words, Christian servanthood and

socio-political servanthood were taught as the same. But
black people recognized the contradictions. So they sang:

> I got a shoe
> You got a shoe
> All of God's chillun got shoe
> When I get to heaven,
> I'm gonna put on my shoe
> I'm gonna walk all over God's heaven.

Even though people outside of the culture may interpret
this message as mere concern for shouting, or the ecstasy
that comes with various forms of spirituality, it in fact was
a challenge to the contradictions under which black people lived. The refrain took an interesting twist:

> Heaven, heaven
> everybody talkin 'bout heaven ain' goin there
> Heaven, heaven
> I'm gonna walk all over God's heaven.[11]

Those Christians who had the power to define the politically oppressed servants ought not to assume that their
earthly political and social powers controlled divine things.
The black person may have been forced into dehumanized
forms of servanthood, but divine retribution was to come.

Interestingly, even though we use the servanthood language with respect to Jesus, we have in effect made him a
part of the bourgeoisie. He has become a privileged person, not unlike the so-called "Christian servants" of the culture of oppressors. They specialize in maintaining their
privileged positions in the church and society, while the
real servants of the world are structurally and systematically
disenfranchised. The real servants are the economically
deprived, the socially ill, the politically impotent, and the

spiritually irrelevant, if in fact not the spiritually empty people. Prevelant images of Jesus seem to escape all these realities. Though he was born in a stable, he has been made royal; he is king of kings. Though he was a Jew, all traces of his Jewishness have been erased. Though he died the common death of a criminal, his agony, suffering and pain have been eliminated. We have created a "sweet Jesus."

A black pastor summed up these ideas when veiwing the stained glass windows recently installed in his church. He said:

> The white church has erased the pain from the
> face of Jesus. He does not suffer. The crucifixion
> is a painful experience. We show the pain, the
> agony, the suffering. It's the face of the black
> man—the face of black people.[12]

The faces on the windows of his church are the faces of the real servants of the world.

I argue that our servanthood language existentially functions as a deceptive tactic to keep non-dominant culture peoples and the non-privileged of the dominant culture complacent. Thus, our white Jesus, the Jesus of the dominant culture, escapes the real tragedy of servanthood. But oppressed peoples do not.

Being among neither the dominant culture nor the privileged class, again, black women and other non-white women, because of their triple jeopardy, are three times removed from the image of Jesus and the image of God. In effect, I argue (as others have done) that Jesus has been conveniently made in the image of white oppressors. William Jones some years ago asked the question,"Is God a White Racist?"[13] Feminists have asked, "Is God/Jesus a male chauvinist pig?" When poor people ask "Why, Lord?" they are asking, "Is God/Jesus for the rich and against the poor?" All of these oppressive conceptions about God/Jesus are reinforced by our imagery and symbols, including language. What is needed is a challenge to Christian theology at the points of its racist, sexist, and servant languages, all of which are contrary to the real message of Jesus Christ.

Womanist Jesus: the mutual struggle for liberation

What we find in the experiences of African American women is a process of mutual liberation: Jesus was liberating or redeeming African American women as African American women were liberating or redeeming Jesus. The Jesus of African American women has suffered the triple bondage of imprisonment. Jesus has been held captive to the sin of patriarchy (sexism), to the sin of white supremacy (racism), and to the sin of privilege (classism). As such, Jesus has been used to keep women in their proper place and blacks meek, mild, and docile in the face of brutal forms of dehumanization, and he has also been used to insure the servility of servants. African American women heard twice (and sometimes three times) the mandate "Be subject..., for it is sanctioned by Jesus and ordained by God...." Consequently, they (African American women and Jesus) have suffered from the sins of racism, sexism and classism.

However, in spite of this oppressive indoctrination, Jesus Christ has been a central figure in the lives of African American women. They obviously experienced Jesus in ways different from what was intended by the teachings and preachings of white oppressors. Four symbols demonstrate how African American women were able to liberate Jesus as Jesus liberated them:
- Jesus as co-sufferer
- Jesus as equalizer

- Jesus means freedom
- Jesus as liberator

Jesus as co-sufferer. Chief among black people's experiences of Jesus was that he was a divine co-sufferer, who empowered them in situations of oppression. For Christian African American women of the past, Jesus was a central point of reference. For despite what was taught them, they were able to identify with Jesus, because they felt that Jesus identified with them in their sufferings. There was mutual suffering. Just like them, Jesus suffered and was persecuted undeservedly. Jesus' sufferings culminated on the cross. African-American women's cross experiences were constant in their daily lives—the abuses physical and verbal, the acts of dehumanization, the pains, the sufferings, the loss of families and friends and the disruption of communities. But because Jesus Christ was not a mere man, but God incarnate, African American women, in these sufferings, connected with the divine. This connection was maintained through their religious life—their prayer tradition and their song tradition. Their prayers were conversations with one who "walked dat hard walk up Calvary and ain't weary but to tink about we all dat way."[14] The connection was also evidenced by the song tradition in which one could lament, "Nobody knows the trouble I see...but Jesus...."

Jesus as equalizer. African American women had been told twice that their inferiority and inequality were a part of the nature of things. They, along with African American men, were taught that they were created to be the servant class for those in control. They were not to preach (in the case of women, and black men in some traditions), and they were to acknowledge their place as a part of God's providence. But African American women experienced Jesus as a great equalizer, not only in the white world, but in the black world as well. And so they would argue that the crucifixion was for universal salvation in its truest sense, not just for male salvation, or for white salvation. Jesus came and died, no less for the woman as for the man, no less for blacks as for whites. Jarena Lee, in the last century said:

> If the man may preach, because the Saviour died for him, why not the woman? Seeing he died for her also. Is he not a whole saviour, instead of a half one? as those who hold it wrong for a woman to preach, would seem to make it appear.[15]

Because Jesus Christ was for all, he in fact equalizes them and renders human oppressive limitations invalid.

Jesus means freedom. Perhaps no one better than Fannie Lou Hamer articulates black women's understanding of Jesus in relation to freedom. She takes us a bit further than the equality language by challenging our understanding of, and desire for mere equality. She said:

> I couldn't tell nobody with my head up I'm fighting for equal right[s] with a white man, because I don't want it. Because if what I get, got to come through lynching, mobbing, raping, murdering, stealing and killing, I didn't want it, because it was a shocking thing to me, I couldn't hardly sit down.[16]

We are challenged to move beyond mere equality to freedom. Freedom is the central message of Jesus Christ and the gospel, and is concisely summarized in Luke 4:18:

> The spirit of the Lord is upon me because I have been anointed to announce good news to the poor, release for prisoners, and recovery of sight

for the blind; to let the broken victims go free, to proclaim the year of the Lord's favor.

Based upon her reading of this text, Hamer's consistent challenge to the American public was that to be a follower of Jesus Christ was to be committed to the struggle for freedom.

Jesus the liberator. The liberation activities of Jesus empower African American women to be significantly engaged in the process of liberation. Sojourner Truth was empowered, so much so that when she was asked by a preacher if the source of her preaching was the Bible, she responded, "No honey, can't preach from de Bible—can't read a letter." Then she explained, "When I preaches, I has jest one text to preach from, an' I always preaches from this one. My text is, 'When I found Jesus!'" In this sermon Sojourner Truth talks about her life, from the time her parents were brought from Africa and sold, to the time that she met Jesus within the context of her struggles for dignity and liberation for black people and women.[17] The liberation message of Jesus provided grounding for the liberation and protest activities of such persons as Sojourner Truth and many other women activists.

Both white women and black women have re-thought their understandings of Jesus Christ. They have done so against all odds. For they (both) live in the context of patriarchy, which has enabled men to dominate theological thinking and church leadership. Black women continue to suffer from the sin of white supremacy, wherein it is believed that the theological task belongs to whites. In the midst of all this, women have emerged to say that women's experiences (African American women, Hispanic women, Native American women and white women) must be taken seriously. Even if men refuse to do so, women must forge ahead.

Notes

1. Bert Lowenberg and Ruth Bogin, eds., *Black Women in Nineteenth Century American Life: Their Words, Their Thoughts, Their Feelings* (University Park, PA: The Pennsylvania State University Press, 1976).

2. Ntozake Shange, *For Colored Girls Who Have Considered Suicide When the Rainbow is Enuf* (New York: Macmillan Publishing Co., 1975), 43.

3. Sheila Collins, *A Different Heaven and Earth* (Valley Forge, PA: Judson Press, 1974), 51.

4. Elizabeth Dodson Gray, *Patriarchy as a Conceptual Trap* (Wellesley, MA: Roundtable Press, 1982), 17.

5. Jacquelyn Grant, *White Women's Christ and Black Woman's Jesus* (Atlanta, GA: Scholars Press, 1989).

6. Joel Kovel, *White Racism: A Psychohistory* (New York: Columbia University Press, 1984), x.

7. C. Eric Lincoln, *Race, Religion, and the Continuing American Dilemma* (New York: Hill and Wang, 1984), 11-12.

8. Randall Bailey, "Beyond Identification: The Use of Africans in Old Testament Poetry and Narratives," in *Stormy the Road We Trod*, ed. Cain Hope Felder (Minneapolis: Augsburg/ Fortress, 1991), 180.

9. Joseph Johnson, "The Need for a Black Christian Theology," *Journal of Interdenominational Theological Center 2* (Fall, 1974): 25.

10. There were several catechisms taught to slaves. See Albert J. Rabateau, *Slave Religion* (New York: Oxford University Press, 1978), 163.

11. This was a song I learned in my childhood. For a variation on the same theme, see Thomas R. Frazier, ed., *Afro-American History: Primary Sources* (Atlanta: Harcourt, Brace and World, Inc., 1970), 93.

12. Matthew Johnson, Interview on April 10, 1992 at Institutional Baptist Church, Greensboro, North Carolina.

13. William James, *Is God a White Racist?* (New York: Anchor Doubleday, 1973).

14. Harold A. Carter, *The Prayer Tradition of Black People* (Valley Forge, PA: Judson Press, 1976), 49.

15. Jerena Lee, *Religious Experiences and Journals of Mrs. Jerena Lee* (Philadelphia, PA: 1849), 15-16.

16. Robert Wright, "Interviews with Fannie Lou Hamer," August 9, 1968, from the Civil Rights Documentation Project, Moorland-Springarn Research Center, Howard University, Washington, D.C.

17. Olive Gilbert, *Sojourner Truth: Narrative and Book of Life* (1850 and 1875; reprint ed., Chicago: Johnson Publishing Co., Inc., 1970), 119.

Who Do You Say Jesus Is? Christological Reflections from a Hispanic Woman's Perspective

MARINA HERRERA

First I wish to place myself on the continuum of women theologians, observers, interpreters and practitioners of religion who abundantly dot the Christian tradition. I want to state at the outset that I am not a feminist theologian; maybe feminine and Americanist would best describe me. In my mind, the word feminist conjures up a political, historical perspective that aims primarily at overcoming *sexism*. I am convinced, however, that sexism is but one minor piece of what ails our Christian culture today. I have suffered at the hands of "patriarchal *racist* matriarchs" and have seen the devastating effects of racism on others enough to know that the sins of our "hierarchical patriarchs" are more encompassing than the North American feminist critique seems to indicate.

In this essay, my aim is not to make the man Jesus more acceptable to women who are dissatisfied with the sexist attitude of the Church, nor to find within the tradition those elements that can be redeemed and reappropriated in order to make the images of God and Jesus more palatable for our language-conscious modern women. My goal is, with the lenses of my inter-cultural, inter-racial, inter-denominational, and inter-class experiences, to engage in an exercise that will allow me to see Jesus in fresh ways and be challenged anew by the demands of his call to take up our cross. In this fashion I hope to explicate once more the relevance of his message of love to our day and troubled times.

I am certain that Jesus, his life, his message and his actions and above all his suffering, death and resurrection have paradigmatic value; but I must confess at the outset that I am also certain that the Christian churches, particularly my Catholic tradition which I know best, have paid lip service to the implications of that message for the way we relate to each other and to our world. The message of Jesus has been well dissected, expounded on with clarity, eloquence and power; it has not been practiced with justice, nor with love.

My search to answer the question, "Who do you say I am?" is born then from an attempt to use zoom lenses to see things our fathers and mothers in the faith could not see, given the optics through which they viewed the world and understood their relationships with others, especially those of other races and traditions. Three interconnecting lenses have aided my search: first, an attempt to see how our forefathers in faith were mistaken not only in their assessments of women, but also in their neglect of, and violence toward races and religions other than their own; second, a re-construction of the social and political world of Jesus; and finally, the devotional and academic accounts of Jesus' life by non-Western authors. I will use all three of these as I try to reconstruct for you my personal journey in identifying Jesus.

Childhood reflections

One of the first prayers that Spanish speaking children learn to say goes like this:

Jesusito de mi vida,
Tú eres niño como yo;
Por eso te *quiero* tanto Y te doy mi corazón.

Which can be translated as:

Dear little Jesus,
You're just a child like me;
Therefore I love you so and I give you my heart.

It is important to note for those who are not Spanish
speakers that just as Spanish has two forms of the verb to
be (*ser* and *estar*), it has two forms for the verb to love
(*amar* and *querer*). In English you can use the word *love* for
everything that you like in a special way. In Spanish we do
not interchange the two. We cannot say, for example, "*Amo
a mi carro*" (I love my car) or "*Amo a mi perro*" (I love my
dog). In English, we can say with the same breath "I love
my God and my dog" In Spanish, we cannot. We reserve
the verb *amar* for God and for a spouse or lover. All other
persons are *queridos* which is, in some ways, more material—it implies you want them for yourself. *Querer* is the verb
that signifies to want or to wish.

From my earliest prayers, Jesus emerged as someone
quite separate and distinct from God. Jesus was one *to
want* to imitate and follow because he was a child like me,
but I reserved my love for God. In my early experience,
God was never referred to in prayer by using the masculine pronoun. The word *Dios* was always used. In the earliest image of God that I can recall, God was a hand which
could be masculine or feminine. Perhaps the hand is the
body part that least reflects gender. I never saw a blue-eyed
God with a white beard until I came to the United States in
my late teenage years.

The second awareness of Jesus' identity came in my early adolescence when I learned a poem by Lope de Vega:

No me mueve mi Dios para quererte el cielo que me
    tienes prometido.
Ni me mueve el infierno tan temido para dejar por
    eso de ofenderte.
Tu me mueves Señor,
Muéveme el verte clavado en una cruz yescarnecido;
Muéveme el ver tu cuerpo tan herido;
Muévenme tus afrentas y tu muerte.
Muéveme en fin tu amor de tal manera que aunque
    no hubiera cielo yo te amara y aunque no
    hubiera hubiera infierno te temiera.
No me tienes que dar porque te quiera porque
    aunque lo que espero no esperara, lo mismo que
    te quiero te quisiera.

This translation is my own:

The heaven you promised, O God,
does not move me to love you.
The much feared hell does not move me nor stop me
    from offending you.
You move me, O Lord, seeing you nailed to a cross
    and reviled;
I am moved by the sight of your wounded body;
I am moved by your sufferings and your death.
Finally, I am so moved by your love
that even if there were no heaven
I would love you,
and if there were no hell I would fear you.
You do not need to offer me anything for me to love
    you,
for even if I did not expect what I hope for
my love would be as great as it is now.

A painting of Jesus on the cross, graphically depicting the powerlessness and pain of the moment, accompanied the prayer. The poet does not mention the Church as the mediator between God and the person. The relationship to God, as experienced in the utmost love expressed by Jesus' passion and death are mediated by the power of the event itself. There is no dogma, no creed, no law that can surpass the power of a suffering man-God, who had assumed his powerlessness to show the extent of God's mercy and love.

My relationship to Jesus as an adolescent was one in which I had power and strength just as Mary in the Pietà scene is the one who can make things happen, when the lifeless body of her Son is left to her to care for and bury. Because my spiritual formation was influenced by Carmelite mystical spirituality, I spent many hours of reflection and prayerful meditation on Jesus' passion. I became aware that all the men in those scenes left much to be desired: Judas' betrayal, Peter's denial, sleeping male disciples, Herod's indecision, and Pilate's evasion of responsibility. With the exception of Simon of Cyrene, the tradition focuses on the courage of the women: the compassion of Veronica, those who came to express their disapproval with their tears only to hear Jesus' rebuke, and the Marys who continued to be present even after there was nothing more to do but to keep alive the memory of a man they had come to love by paying him the customary post-burial tributes.

Those images of Jesus—first as a child and then as a powerless executed man—shaped my sense of the role of women in the world. That role, as a teenager, and now as mostly an "ager," has not changed much. When faced with the suffering that people inflict upon one another, women are called to comfort, to heal, to pick up the pieces, to bury the dead, to confront and to shame with our tears the inhumanity of injustice and violence. We are called to keep memories alive and to be the main actors in the after-death drama, the heralds of the good news of the empty tomb. There is life after death!

The holy cards of Jesus that were part of my child-hood not only never pictured a powerful figure, they never showed a blond and blue-eyed Jesus. A black or brown haired man with olive complexion and a Mediterranean look (which probably resembled more the real Jewish Jesus) was standard. Thus, it was a surprise for me to find the glorified Christ taught and promoted in the United States. It was here that I was first exposed to Jesus as King and Ruler, the triumphant male images that feminist theologians find restrictive. I have never been able to make these images of Jesus or others part of my spirituality.[1] This "failure" of my inculturation into the American religious scene was due to these two factors: first, the images I brought to this country were well imbedded and developed in my religious psyche; and second, due to my less than adequate knowledge of English, I was not affected by the more sexist, intellectualized images of the glorified Christ of the northern European and American traditions.

When I later came to read about the misconceptions of Aquinas regarding women or the Augustinian exegesis of the Genesis account, I only saw them as vestiges of past understandings that, as far as I was concerned, had no applicability to me or to my world. Just as I would not take issue with geocentric cosmologists prior to the invention of the telescope, I found it anachronistic to take issue with Augustine or Aquinas. They never diminished my sense of worth as a human being nor took away the sense of my power as woman to create, heal, nurture, and pick up the pieces of the disasters we inflict on ourselves and each other. These images did not and could not prevent me from altering relations, burying the dead, and proclaiming good news at the sight of empty tombs and shattered hopes. Hence, never have I felt the need to spend time or energy showing how mistaken our forefathers in the faith were.

Those stereotypical characteristics assigned to men and women, which we are trying so hard to overcome, have emerged from pre-science, pre-modern technology. Without the tools of modern science and technology, it is impossible to see the complementarity of men and women in the procreative processes. Unaided by the knowledge provided by microscopes, internal photography and chromosomal composition of the human body, an observer of mammalian anatomy and the sexual acts of animals will view the male as more active than the female. The male's action will appear to be assertive while the woman's appears to be receptive. The woman's contribution to the procreative process is completely outside the purview of the naked eye. Therefore I am not given to railing against the misguided patriarchal conceptions of women. I have become more interested in learning to interpret those men and women, who by their approach, tone, and style of relating reflect the more balanced scientific understanding of male and female as unique, distinct and indispensable contributors to the human quest whether in procreative processes or throughout the entire gamut of human activity. When I sense that men or women within a Christian ecclesiastical setting are operating from understandings that originated in the hierarchical, classist, sexist, racist and age-ist modes established by our Greco-Roman ancestors, I do what Jesus suggested to his followers when he sent them two by two: "But when you enter a town and are not welcomed, go into its streets and say, 'Even the dust of your town that sticks to our feet we wipe off against you. Yet be sure of this: The kingdom of God is near'" (John 10:10-11). This is one of the aspects of Jesus' message that

I find has a new meaning for me—his refusal to be confrontational, his refusal to eradicate evil no matter what the cost. Jesus did not believe in violence, whether verbal or otherwise.

A new assessment of Christian praxis

The closing years of this century accompanied by the events marking the quincentenary of the arrival of Europeans in this continent provide a fitting platform from which to view, evaluate and critique the fruits of Western Christianity. There is nothing more revealing of personal self-understanding than facing the unknown. In this experience one must name, relate, and incorporate into one's universe of meanings, the meaning and significance of others who unexpectedly intrude into one's awareness. This is the special moment we have available today. By looking at the process that started five hundred years ago, and considering the ways in which avowed Christian nations confronted the novelty of the American continent and its peoples, I have gained a humbling realization of the insignificance of the sexist crimes of our fathers in contrast with the racist ones of the Christian West toward the natives of this continent and toward the Africans enslaved and brought here.

Studying the disputes regarding the human nature of the Natives of this continent and the legal claims that European Christian churches and governments concocted in order to expropriate the new lands, enslave and decimate their peoples, and subject millions more from other lands to the degradations of slavery has confirmed my convictions. The vision of the world and the various sciences supporting this vision were simply inadequate to all that the Europeans found when arriving on this continent. We moderns have still not courageously applied a critique

analogous to the feminist critique to the Eurocentric vision
of the world that upholds and maintains structures of privilege and power for some while negating the dignity of
non-European, non-white, and non-Christian peoples in
even more unacceptable ways than those negating the dignity of Euro-American women. In fact, our socio-economic
structures often coopt feminist women into being accom-
plices to the continued betrayal of non-white, non-
European, and non-Christian women.

My explorations into the events of these 500 years
have convinced me that we are at the end, not only of this
century, but also at the end of the supremacy of a
Eurocentric perspective of the world. A new world reality,
basically shaped by the ethos of the American continent
before Europe scarred it with its search for gold, glory, and
power, is being born. The reflections, writings, and
debates over whether to mourn or to celebrate Columbus
being held across the land are the first hints of this new
birth. This is a time to consider how European philosophy,
law, epistemology, science, and even theology not only
have brought us to the brink of ecological disaster, but also
have continued the injustice between nations. Growing
chasms between the haves and the have-nots, increased
tension between races, and expected violence between
human beings of different sexual orientation may be
attributed to the dualisms confirmed by early European
thought.

For me, what is at stake is the destiny of the planet
and its peoples as we travel in this beautiful blue dot
around the galaxies with a thousand suns. America, the
New World, was invented as the place where the European
Utopia could be fulfilled. Columbus himself was certain
that this was the location of the Garden of Eden, a theory
that persisted well into the seventeenth century.[2] The
Americas today are inhabited by peoples of the entire

globe who have come here in search of a better place, their personal utopia. Here then, we have the opportunity to give shape to a science, philosophy, theology and anthropology reflecting the utopian ideals of all cultures. By seeing themselves in the reformulations of what is the optimal human community all cultures can come to an awareness of their unique and irreplaceable contribution to the human quest and of the totality of the human contribution to the unfolding of the universe with its ultimate meaning. This meaning is not defined by one faith tradition, but defined by all the faith traditions that have proven their durability and vitality. From this perspective, we must cease talking about ecumenism as a dialogue between Christianity and the so-called "world religions," and begin to speak about dialogue with the religions of the world, especially with the ancient ones of our continent and also those that have emerged as the syncretistic response to the intermingling of Christianity with African and Native American spiritualities and cosmologies.

This continent is the result of the convergence for the first time in history of peoples from the entire globe. The Europe of 500 years ago was based on the partial insights of Greco-Roman philosophy and law, forged in constant political and religious wars, that have left us with inadequate understandings of women, children, sexuality, religious experience, the nature of human knowledge and of relations with those of other races. Today, the Americas have assembled the largest cadre of scholars from all races, religious and philosophical traditions who can empower us to see the biases of one perspective.

In order to give birth to a new Christology, we must begin with a thorough critique of our Western tradition. This critique should not be fashioned from the feminist viewpoint only, because the feminist viewpoint, in itself, does not encompass enough of what needs reworking. An

"Americanist critique"—done by the people of this continent, men and women, young and old, Natives, European,
African, and Asian descendants—*must be a critique of all
things European,* including the Westernization of Jesus and
his message and the assumption that such Westernization
is the only valid interpretation of the salvific event of his
life and death. This critique must ponder the effects (both
positive and negative) of European science, philosophy,
anthropology, politics, law, and theology (ecclesiology,
Christology and ethics) on the natural form and resources
of this continent as well as on its original inhabitants, on
those forced to come here in slave ships, and on those who
never were or never will be because of the policies of
extermination and subjugation by our European fathers.

It is difficult for children to find fault with their parents, especially if they perceive them as good and caring.
But this for me is the meaning of Jesus' injunction that we
must leave fathers and mothers if we are to accomplish the
work he would have us accomplish. This Americanist critique is in many respects already underway from scientific
labs to schools of liberation and creation spirituality.
Women, however, need to enter into it fully and broaden
their scope beyond those issues of sexism that are our
main agenda today. We women must become as sensitive
to the devastating impact of Eurocentric notions of the
world and of human existence on the rest of humankind as
we have become to the limitations of sexist language. The
task that lies ahead is to understand the shortcomings of
our Eurocentric heritage to undertake a study of the cultural, religious, artistic and technological riches of the cultures of this hemisphere. Only in this fashion shall we
begin to create a new synthesis of human meanings which
will facilitate the true unfolding of a New World incorpo-
rating all the continents, a New World that is not yet.

The feminine–Americanist critique

The scientific and technological critique has been undertaken by the ecologically minded and the pacifists who have slowly but surely made us see the futility and self-destructiveness of many Western scientific tenets. We have seen that progress in almost every field of science and technology has produced undesirable effects. We choke on pollution, we fear another Chernobyl and the depletion of the ozone layer, and we hope the itinerant barges and trucks of garbage will not find a resting place in our city. We are puzzled by the resources we spend in sustaining the life of those who are too ill, or too afraid to go on to the next life, when at the same time we use the most contorted feats of logic and human rights to deprive the unborn from even a glimpse of this messy, but beautiful and unique (and not disposable) world that God has given us. The feminine contribution must be one that places women and our procreative powers at the service of life for future generations of human beings. Women must speak out for the careful and reverent use of our non-renewable natural resources, for the uncompromising defense of the environment, and for the support of scientific research that does not inflict damage on any creature.

The critique of European philosophy and epistemology has also been progressing rapidly as the result of research into the brain, artificial intelligence and computer science. The advent of the computer can only be compared to the creation of the telescope and the microscope in its ability to enable us to see hidden worlds. The telescope provided a glimpse of the universe beyond a starry night. We have seen our smallness and discovered earth to be a grain of dust in the universal ocean of the cosmos. Remember the theological debates that Copernicus' discovery caused! The microscope has afforded vistas of the

complexity of all matter and of our kinship with trees and
rocks and snails. And now the computer shows that the
heretofore distinctly human and unique ability of the mind
to do logical calculations has been shredded to bits by the
super computers performing 50 million calculations and
classifications in a split second. We know that the computer is powerful because the human mind created it. Our
power does not lie in our ability to solve logical problems
or mathematical calculations. These can well be left to this
extension of our senses. We now are beginning to perceive
a whole new significance for the place of memory and the
instant recognition and connectivity skills mediated by the
human eye as perhaps even more uniquely human than
logic and reason. The most difficult tasks that computer
scientists face is how to enable computers to instantly recognize the letter "A," for example, no matter how fancy or
how clumsy its shape. The optical character recognition
programs to date, when compared to human recognition
abilities, have but an infinitesimal ability to identify correctly letters presented to them, no matter their shape or
the kind of paper, clean or dirty, they are written on.[3]

Connectivity, memory and instant visual recognition
skills of millions of bits of data are among the human characteristics well developed by some of the native populations of this continent and by women. A book of eye exercises I recently used mentioned the almost mythical ability
of Native Americans to see long distance objects and recognize them correctly before any of their European
friends or foes could do so. The feminine contribution
here is most pronounced because having been subjected to
the inadequacies of the patriarchal educational system for
a shorter period of time, and only in some areas, we have
continued to develop our ability to connect, to remember,
and to see, both through the senses and through the mind,
that which went beyond the external expressions of

women's minds as presented in books.[4]

The theological critique of European thought is well under way in the theologies of liberation, creation spirituality, eco-theology, and feminism. The books and articles by Gustavo Gutierrez, Jon Sobrino, Leonardo Boff, Matthew Fox, and many United States feminists, now joined by some Latin American women, such as Elsa Tamez and Aracely de Rochietti, Consuelo del Prado and Ivone Gebara, to mention only a few, are keeping religious publishing houses afloat at a time when European conceived theological treatises have become the interest of an ever narrower segment of readership.

There is no greater place in need of an Americanist critique than the area of anthropology. There is no clearer expression of the shortcomings of Western philosophy, theology, and understandings of the human person than in an argument of Juan Ginés de Sepúlveda, scholastic philosopher at the Spanish Court at the time Europeans found this continent. When trying to describe the nature of the populations flourishing in this part of the world for millennia, he concluded: "The Indians, when compared to the Spaniards, are as children to adults, women to men, beasts to humans." Ginés de Sepúlveda was known for his ability to express in understandable prose the principles of Aristotelian philosophy which were the basis of his evaluation of the nature of the inhabitants of this continent. His statement can be changed to include Africans, who, unfortunately for them, had not yet found a defender for their rights as the Indians had in the person of Bartolomé de las Casas to whom Ginés de Sepúlveda had presented his conclusions.

For this anthropological critique, we go to intercultural studies to see that *different* does not mean *inferior* and better weapons do not necessarily insure survival. Having the "smarts" to create the ultimate destructive weapon may be the surest sign of the ultimate stupidity. We are being confronted with the failure of Western wisdom in many simple but crucial areas of human life, such as nutrition, life and death, sex and recreation. Rice, beans, fruits, and roots are healthier for us than red meat, candy bars, and chips, which consistently diminish our pockets and our health. Death with dignity at seventy may be much better than death at ninety, if one is unable to function. Each child born viewed as a potential bread winner is more humane and Christian than impeding millions of births for fear of not being able to care for them in lonely superabundance. Sex is a dangerous and awesome human activity which can be a weapon of destruction and disease unless regulated by controls and perimeters which place it at the service of humanity.

We do not need to see the episode of the "Barbarian West" in the recently aired PBS series to admit and recognize that the West's overwhelmingly prevalent mode of behavior toward "the other" has been conquest, domination, expropriation and subjugation. From the time Alexander the Great extended his empire by ransacking all the way to India, to the fateful night of January 21, 1991 when so called "smart bombs" were dropped by the thousands on Iraqi targets, death and destruction by westerners has been rampant. It has been an eye-opener for me to discover the direct kinship lines between two war generals of European roots separated by time and nationality but linked in the same inner conviction that their cause is just, that the evil they are about to stamp out is more evil and immoral than the evils and immorality of the acts they are about to undertake against the enemy. Reading Hernan Cortés and General Schwarzkopf's speeches side by side has confirmed for me the immorality of war, whether for ideological or religious reasons.

Europe and most of its wise men of the sixteenth century were too full of self-importance, too wrapped up in their own self-interests, too restricted by the limitations imposed on the human mind by the Greek canons of truth and beauty, too entrenched in the unfair practices of Roman law. Embedded in its society was the religious intransigence of Hellenized Christianity with its hierarchical understanding of this world and of the world of the spirits. Sixteenth century Europeans were simply not capable of understanding, appreciating and learning the reality which was this continent, its geological, natural, and human marvels. *They could not and did not discover America.*

I like to think that we are at the beginning of a period in human thought and awareness similar to the European Renaissance, fueled as it was by the discovery of ancient Greek and Roman sources. This time, however, the Renaissance will have world-wide impact if we come to grips with the meaning of this continent and of all that is contained here in its ancient cultures and civilizations, its animal and plant life. Europeans did not discover America. They covered up America and its people—even buried enormous segments of America and its people—in fear, perhaps, of being overshadowed by the splendor they found here. This Americanist critique of things European by all genders, races and creeds must have as its first goal the true discovery of what the hemisphere and its natural and human resources represent for the entire well-being of the globe. Only insofar as that real discovery is achieved will we have set the stage for a new evangelization of the continent, yet to take place. And before that reappraisal can begin all Western institutions, ecclesiastical, governmental, educational, and economic, must make atonement. Our fathers sinned, our mothers sinned, and we have sinned. The feminine contribution here will be greatest if we accept our role as healers, buriers of the dead and proclaimers of the good news that there is life after death.

The empty tombs and the burnt-out shells of our cities must force us to look beyond ourselves in recognition that alone we can do nothing, but with God who strengthens us we can do all things.

Who do you say I am?

In the context of these reflections born from my studies related to the quincentenary, I have asked myself the question being posed to us today: "*Who is the Jesus I believe in?*"

I am not particularly enamored with the title of Jesus as "Son of Man" and whatever mysterious quality it may have had in its original form. But I do not think that Jesus as the "Human One" conveys the dynamic relational quality which is the core of Jesus' uniqueness. Jesus as the "Human One," as proposed by the translators who worked on a non-sexist version of the New Testament for the World Council of Churches, is not broad or encompassing enough of all that Jesus is and of all that is contained in the sexist-sounding title "Son of Man." In this latter phrase we have to go beyond the two male words and see the underlying context that they represent. The word "son" is not only a noun describing males, it is a term that implies a relationship, a way of being part of a family. The son in every culture has a specific set of responsibilities, duties, and privileges. In the Jewish culture of two thousand years ago, being son meant a specific set of rules and norms of etiquette that ensured the continued survival of the family and the harmonious unfolding of family life. I prefer to think of "Son of Man" not as a title that merely stresses or highlights Jesus' maleness, but as one which underscores his relationship, duties, responsibilities and privileges as first born of the New Dispensation.

I cannot read the Gospels without realizing that if

Jesus means anything new or different it has to be in his way of being present to the entire community in which his life evolved. Emmanuel or "God-with-us" says best who Jesus is for me. This title stresses the way he was present to everything—water and rocks, flowers and birds, sinners and saints, poor and rich, young and old, males and females, the sick and the well.

Jesus was non-possessive—he never claimed an attachment to anything including his mother, his town, his own ideas of who he was.

Jesus was forgiving, even of those who tortured and killed him. What a great quality for us women to cultivate—to forgive the sexist patriarchs, those who have oppressed us but also those who have allowed us to flourish, publish our articles and our books and even pay to hear us lecture!

Jesus was non-paternalistic. He did not feel sorry for us women. He spoke harshly to his mother, to the Canaanite woman, to the women who felt sorry for him on the way to Calvary, and to Mary when she complained about Martha. That is the true sign of a person who sees another on an equal footing—the willingness to be challenging, if necessary to be harsh in order to establish the validity of one's position. Jesus did not speak kindly out of condescension or out of his belief that the women were defenseless or ignorant.

Jesus respected women's roles and their territories. The story of the woman at the well is the clearest example of how he accepted a woman's role and admitted his dependence on her tools for drawing water from the well. Once Jesus had acknowledged that she'd call the shots and he was in need, he proceeded to establish his own uniqueness by suggesting that his water takes away thirst forever and that his well never runs dry. What else is new! Now, each has established a certain identity, and the conversation can proceed into serious matters. He did not assume that because she was a poor woman who drew water from the well, she was incapable of understanding the deeper realities of life which he wanted to talk about. He also grasped the fact that she would make a better proclaimer of his message among her people than he or his disciples.

Jesus was not over-protective of women. He allowed his mother to be concerned with his escapade in Jerusalem when he was still a young lad. He did not prevent her seeing his suffering; and, he allowed her to stand by the cross without shielding her from the drama of his torture and death. He even loudly turned down the compliment of the woman who called out from the crowd: "Blessed are the breasts that nursed you."

Because I see Jesus primarily as "God-with-us," I am not particularly moved or inspired or challenged by the notion that Jesus is the *Logos* of God as the tradition has upheld, or by his being the *Sophia* of God, as has been suggested by Elizabeth Johnson. Both descriptors derive from a specific epistemological and philosophical structure that place knowledge above love. This is not surprising, given the tendency of the Western mind to underscore the value of mental processes above all other human capabilities. It is also the North American fascination with knowledge and the privileges it imparts. In a recent book, Harold Bloom analyzes religions derived from Christianity and born in the United States, and suggests that they all rest on gnostic principles. He also suggests that all religions as practiced in the U.S. have gnostic tendencies. Reviewer Jack Miles sees Bloom's work as a valid exposé of "the eccentricity of our spiritual center."[5] These gnostic tendencies are affirmed whenever we try to give Jesus new titles that express his identity in terms of his mental or intellectual uniqueness. We need to rely on Jesus' self-description: "I am the good shepherd, the vinedresser, the householder." These descriptions emphasize relational qualities, not the intellect.

I do not think that Jesus ever hinted at having specialized knowledge. His saying: "I know the Father and he knows me," is expressive of his special relation to the divinity, and has to be understood in terms of the more encompassing meaning of "knowing" in the Jewish tradition. When looking for a successor, Jesus did not ask Peter how good a fisherman he was, or how well he knew the prophets or the law. Rather his question pointed to an overriding concern for the relationships he hoped his followers would have: "Peter, do you love me?" Not only once did he ask, but three times. How often have you—especially those of you who work in the Church, from pastors to deans of theology schools—been been asked that question? Might "Do you love him?" be the all important question during a job interview for Christian ministry? The scriptural passage in which the question appears has been traditionally interpreted as the key passage illustrating the primacy of Peter and of the Church of Rome. I see in it a special moment for understanding the way in which Jesus assesses leadership potential for his followers. Leadership is not based on knowledge, but it is based on love. Jesus was not interested in having someone who could teach, preach, heal, raise funds or organize. He was interested in the acid test of the person's relational character—Peter's ability to love.

To summarize this tendency of Jesus, I like to think that Jesus is above all a linker and not a ranker. Linkers persuade others to give up their self-appointed importance, their arrogance, or their holier-than-thou attitudes. Recall the story of the woman caught in adultery. Linkers look for relational qualities as all important among those who shall do the work of the kingdom. Rankers prefer to have those whose knowledge places them at the top of their ranked classes. In community building rankers tend to work out of hierarchical, systematic, isolationist, categorical, and dogmatic structures of reality. Linkers work out of relational, communitarian, integrative, tentative, artistic, spontaneous structures of reality.

Our images of God do not need to be feminine before we women can feel truly human. First we must alter our image of each other and then our images of God will change. Somehow, there is a misunderstanding in the writings of some feminists. They argue that a feminine image of God will make women fully human and in turn will promote the equality of the sexes. However, this is not the way language works or is created. We create language to express new realities that emerge in the process of manipulating or transforming our world and our relations. We do not become less sexist or racist after we have renamed God or imaged the divine in a different colored face. We do not model ourselves after a God whom we have never seen. We model, describe, and define God after ourselves, and after our imperfect understandings of reality. When women treat men as if they too are made in a feminist (less sexist) image of God, when white women treat African, Hispanic, or Native American women not as slaves or servants, but as sisters, then our images of God will change. When we all—whites, blacks, browns, yellows, reds, and greens—hear the cry of the poor or heed the cry of those who are not allowed to utter even their first cry, we will transform our relations with each other and then our images of God, the Church, and Jesus will be transformed, too. We must change our relations with each other and with all of creation. Only then will the vocabulary to designate God and our relations to the divine change.

In reflecting on the events of the quincentenary, contrasting my images of Jesus with those of the mainline United States religious tradition, and examining how easy it is for me to name something that presents no problems with my preconceptions of the world, I have been convinced that if Christianity is to emerge as a force for change in favor of all humanity, we theologians, and especially we women theologians, have the responsibility to broaden our scope. We must hear the cries of all those segments of our society, indeed our world, who are victimized by the hierarchical patrimony that relegates all that is not white, male, mainline Christian, and did not originate with Europeans and their descendants to a marginal place in the schema of things. We must set about changing structures and ways of relating, creating the dynamics for exchanges that are not sexist, racist, classist, or ageist and then the words to designate Jesus and God will surely follow naturally. Divine grace is more than race and extends beyond maleness. Redemption is more than education and degrees. Salvation is more than suburbanization. Hell is not living in a color-filled neighborhood, and heaven is not an unending shopping-spree at the supermall. We must dare to unceasingly proclaim the suffering face of Jesus as the reflection of our sinful refusal to accept, rejoice in, and celebrate our magnificent diversity as the outpouring of God's creativity.

Notes

1. During my years as a religious I was never inspired or convinced by the bridal imagery which was promoted in the convent and fostered among young novices. The bridal image of the Scriptures was for me clearly one which applied allegorically, in the tradition of the Spanish mystics Juan de la Cruz and Teresa de Avila, to the soul and God and not the religious female as bride of Jesus, the Bridegroom. I do not even accept as appropriate the image of Jesus the bridegroom and the Church the bride. My reasons fall outside the scope of this presentation and may

be better explored in the context of another crucial question that women theologians need to wrestle with: what is the Church, understood in a non-patriarchal, non-hierarchical, non-sexist, non-classicist, non-ageist and non-racist world view?

2. A book by Antonio León Pinelo from Lima appeared in the period 1650-1656 with the title, *El pardiso en el Nuevo Mundo. Comentario apologético, historia natural y peregrina de las Indias Occidentales.* It was reissued in 1943 by the Peruvian Committee of the IV Centenary of the Discovery of the Amazon River, edited by Raúl Porras Barrenechea. In this theory, the Garden of Eden had been located between the Amazon and the Marañon Rivers.

3. Jeremy Campbell, *The Improbable Machine: What New Discoveries in Artificial Intelligence Reveal About How the Mind Really Works* (New York: Touchstone, 1989).

4. Cf. Anne Wilson Schaef, *Women's Reality: An Emerging Female System in a White Male Society* (Minneapolis: Winston Press, 1985).

5. Harold Bloom, *The American Religion. The Emergence of the Post-Christian Nation* (New York: Simon & Schuster, 1992). Reviewed by Jack Miles in "Book World," *Washington Post* (May 17, 1992), 4.

Wisdom Was Made Flesh and Pitched Her Tent Among Us

ELIZABETH A. JOHNSON

Introduction

During Advent in many Christian churches a hymn sung to a haunting melody calls for divine mystery to draw near and rescue captive exiles: "O Come, O Come Emmanuel." The second verse repeats this cry in wisdom language:

> O Come thou Wisdom from on high,
> who orders all things mightily;
> to us the path of knowledge show,
> and teach us in her ways to go.
> Rejoice, rejoice, Emmanuel
> Shall come to thee, O Israel.

I draw attention at the outset to this hymn because it is one of the few traces left in present day use and consciousness of what in scripture, early Christian theology, and medieval mysticism is a pivotal way of speaking about Christ. Who is Wisdom whose approach the community desires, what are her ways, and how is she connected with Jesus the Christ?

The answers to these questions are largely unknown today, and theological education has not hastened to fill the gap. Until quite recently the biblical wisdom tradition has been relegated to a position of minor importance, while the powerful female figure of Wisdom, *Sophia* in Greek, has been ignored. In Christology the pivotal role of this symbol in articulating the meaning of Christ has been forgotten and its continuing use suppressed in favor of the centrality of the Father-Son metaphor.

I would like to propose that wisdom is too valuable a resource to continue to be forgotten. Both the insights and imagery of the wisdom tradition, when interpreted by means of a feminist hermeneutic, offer a way of speaking about Jesus the Christ that can correct the androcentric bias of traditional Christology and shape the community and its engagement with the world in an inclusive, freeing, and relational manner.

Let me be clear: I am not suggesting that the wisdom tradition is a panacea for all that ails us. In its original form it is intensely androcentric, as much as other elements of our intellectual heritage. Some of the most offensive biblical statements about women are found in its pages. But just as the historical books of the Bible yield clues to the equality of women and men and offer glimpses of women as acting subjects of history, even leaders of their people; and, just as the prophetic scrolls deliver a message of liberation that can be reinterpreted today to embrace even women whom the prophets had not intended to include; so too the wisdom tradition can be critically retrieved to yield an inclusive vision of wholeness that can benefit women as well as men, indeed the whole earth.

Let us, then, remember *Sophia,* and learn again to speak about Jesus in the power of her mighty and people-loving spirit. We will deal in turn with four points:

1. Wisdom in the scriptures of Israel
2. Wisdom Christology in the Christian scriptures

3. Untying the knot of sexist Christology
4. Ramifications: social justice, encounter with world religions, and ecological care for the earth.

I. Wisdom in the scriptures of Israel

A. *The wisdom tradition itself.* In the centuries following the Enlightenment there was a tendency among biblical scholars to sideline the wisdom writings in favor of the historical and prophetic books of the Bible. It was alleged that encounter with God's mighty acts in history is at the center of Jewish religious experience, that "Yahwism" is an essential characteristic of Jewish faith, and that therefore the narrative interpretation of salvation history is the primary form of biblical witness.

The wisdom tradition does not easily fit into the type of faith exhibited in the historical and prophetic literature so described, for it has a different way of discerning God's manifestations. It focuses not so much on once-for-all sacred deeds in history, although it remembers these, as on the continuing world of natural, everyday, mundane life, being interested in interpersonal and societal relationships, in nature and its workings, in the meaning of human life and the anguishing problem of suffering. Furthermore, wisdom is not exclusive to Israel but has an affinity with the insights of the sages of Egypt and other advanced cultures of the ancient Near East, and in fact is often borrowed from them. Unlike traditions of law and cult which were preserved and maintained by the priests, wisdom escapes the control of any one group. It does not find its center in the Temple but is given to anyone who searches out the order of creation in order to live in harmony with it.

In recent decades biblical scholars have criticized the way their forebears relegated wisdom to secondary status, arguing that the wisdom tradition reflects a genuine, primary element of biblical faith itself.[1] The narrow track of encounter with God in salvation history is not the only way, indeed for some not even the primary way, that religious experience occurs. People connect with the holy mystery that surrounds their lives as they actually *live* in the world, in the non-heroic moments, in the effort to be decent and just, in puzzling over setbacks and suffering, in appreciating nature, in trying to work out relationships harmoniously, in the gift and task of the everyday—in this, every bit as much as in the peak experiences of personal or community life. Since the whole world is God's creation, life cannot be neatly divided into sacred and profane times or places. Even in its daily-ness, life mediates connections with the mystery of the Holy One, hidden and present. Such is the vision of the wisdom tradition, and it does have the potential to undercut the dualistic opposition between God and the world that plagues classical, patriarchal theology, including its interpretation of Christ.

B. *Wisdom herself.* In the midst of the biblical wisdom writings arises the symbol of myth of Wisdom/Sophia, a female figure of power and care. The biblical picture of her is a composite one, formed of differing presentations in Job and Proverbs (books common to all users of the Bible), and in the deuterocanonical books of Sirach, Baruch and the Wisdom of Solomon (books considered canonical by Catholic and Orthodox but not by Protestant or Jewish communities). Intertestamental literature such as Enoch also contributes to her depiction. Portrayed as sister, mother, bride, hostess, female beloved, woman prophet, teacher, and friend, but above all as divine spirit, Sophia's portrait has its roots in the Great Goddess of the ancient Near Eastern world.[2] Overall, there is no other personification of such depth and magnitude in the entire scriptures of Israel.

Scholarly debate on how to interpret this powerful female figure abounds, not least because various biblical books depict her in differing ways so that no one interpretation can be applied to every verse where Wisdom appears. Thus the arguments: Wisdom is the personification of cosmic order;[3] no, she is the personification of the wisdom sought and learned in Israel's wisdom schools;[4] no, she is a personified way of speaking about God's insight and knowledge;[5] no, she is a hypostasis, a kind of subordinate persona who operates between the transcendent, inaccessible God and those on earth;[6] no, she is the personification of God's own self coming toward the world, dwelling in it, active for its well-being.[7]

Taking the whole wisdom tradition into account, it is this last interpretation that was to bear fruit in Christology as early Christians grew in the realization of what God had done in Jesus Christ. For *Sophia's* creative and saving actions are divine ones. Wisdom texts must be read within their historical religious context, which was (and remains) monotheism. Unless one thinks the Jewish community broke with its faith in one God when writing and receiving the wisdom literature, *Sophia's* functional equivalence with Yahweh requires that she be interpreted as a powerful female symbol of this one God.[8] Thus, to say that *Sophia* is the fashioner of all things, that she delivered Israel from a nation of oppressors, or that her gifts are justice and life is to speak of the transcendent God's relation to the world, of divine nearness and activity and summons. The Wisdom of God in late Jewish thought is simply God, revealing and known.

Consider these facets of her symbol and story:

● Wisdom is utterly elusive and hidden, and cannot be found by human effort alone (Job 28:12-28). But, when lured by her attractiveness, we search for her, then she finds us and reveals herself at will. So one with God is she that she is God's breath, emanation, radiance, very own image (Wis 7:25-26).

• Creative agency is hers, for she exists before the beginning of the world and through her all things are made. The great poem of Proverbs 8:22-31 depicts her playing everywhere in the new world and finding delight among human beings. She is called the "fashioner" or "artisan" (*technitis*) of all things (Wis 7:22, 8:6), and the "mother" of all good things, responsible for their existence and therefore knowing their inmost secrets (Wis 7:12).

• Providential power to arrange the universe harmoniously is hers, for she reaches from end to end of the earth and orders all things well (Wis 8:1). In human society, too, the right order of good governance is grounded on her: "By me kings reign, and rulers decree what is just" (Prov 8:15).

• Redeeming agency is hers, for throughout history human beings "were saved by wisdom" (Wis 9:18). In a stunning series of examples the Wisdom of Solomon recounts Wisdom's saving deeds from Adam to the Exodus, including how she led her people out from a nation of oppressors and brought them through the deep waters of the Red Sea (Wis 10). The verbs "delivered" (she delivered) and "preserved" (she preserved), elsewhere used of divine action, are repeated throughout.

• Wisdom has a spirit that pervades all things, weaving connections and holding everything together. Her spirit is a holy one, intelligent, subtle, mobile, benevolent, steadfast, all powerful: twenty-one attributes in all, or three times the perfect number seven (Wis 7:22-23). With her living, pure spirit she enters into holy souls and makes them friends of God, and prophets (Wis 7:27).

• In her spirit Wisdom accompanies people through thick and thin, through all the raging waters and deserts of hard times (Wis 10:17-18). The later Jewish tradition carried this theme forward in the symbol of the *shekinah,* divine presence who goes with the people into exile, weeps and mourns their grief, suffers with their pain, feels the death even of a criminal who is hanged.[9]

• At every turn Wisdom promises the divine gift of life, signifying shalom, salvation, justice: "whoever finds me finds life" (Prov 8:35). The gift is given in many personal and corporate ways. She enlightens, teaches, guides feet into the way of peace. In a basic gesture of life she nourishes her children and her guests, sending her maidservants to invite all to come, eat of her bread, and drink of her wine (Prov 9:5).

• When corruption creeps in she reproves and corrects, prophesies in robust and stinging terms, and judges wrongdoing (Prov 1:20-33). At the same time, while remaining in herself, she keeps on making all things new (Wis 7:27). Ultimately hers is the victory over evil:

> For she is more beautiful than the sun,
> and excels every constellation of the stars.
> Compared with the light she is found to be superior,
> for day is succeeded by the night,
> but against wisdom evil does not prevail
>   (Wis 7:29-30).

• Wisdom who pervades the entire cosmos seeks a dwelling place among human beings and pitches her tent in Israel (Sir 24:23, where Wisdom is identified with Torah), or comes to dwell among human beings (Bar 3:37). In Sirach's account she flourishes there. By contrast, Enoch develops the theme of *Sophia's* rejection. She goes forth to make her dwelling place among human beings, but finds none. Therefore she withdraws and returns to the heavens (41:1-2).

As even this all too brief scan shows, Wisdom in the scriptures of Israel is simply God: reaching out to the world, forming the beloved community, forever drawing near and passing by. For of whom else can all these things be said? In the context of a monotheistic faith, the wisdom literature celebrates God's gracious goodness in creating and sustaining the world and in electing and saving Israel, and does so in the imagery of a woman. She personifies divine reality; in fact, she *is* a most intense expression of divine presence and activity in the world. It is important to note explicitly that the female symbol of Wisdom is far from the stereotype of the feminine that androcentric thought equates with the reality of women.

The discovery of biblical *Sophia* is watering the roots of much feminist spirituality and language about God today. But we are here to speak about Christ. What is perhaps more fascinating than the wisdom tradition in the scriptures of Israel is the way in which, having incorporated prophetic, apocalyptic, and messianic currents in the years B.C.E., it is used by first-century Christian communities to probe the significance of the crucified prophet from Nazareth.[10]

II. *Wisdom Christology in the Christian scriptures*

In their exuberant effort to interpret their experience of salvation coming from God in Jesus and consequently his ultimate meaning, early Christians ransacked their Jewish religious tradition and the surrounding Hellenistic culture for interpretive elements. Consequently they named him the Messiah/Christ, the Son of Man, Lord, Son of God, Word of God, allowing the meaning of these traditions to interact with his particular history and so shed light on his significance. In a way fraught with importance for later development they also connected him with Wisdom, allowing her symbol and myth to focus and filter his significance. As the trajectory of wisdom Christology shows, Jesus was so closely associated with *Sophia* that by the end of the first century he is presented not only as a wisdom teacher, not only as a child and envoy of *Sophia*, but as an earthly appearance of Wisdom in person, the incarnation of *Sophia* herself.[11]

Paul is the first to write down the connection, noting "we preach Christ crucified, a stumbling block to the Jews and folly to the Gentiles, but to those who are called, both Jews and Greeks, Christ the power of God and the wisdom of God (1 Cor 1:22-24). Christ crucified, the wisdom of God.[12] Here is the transvaluation of values so connected with the ministry, death and resurrection of Jesus: divine *Sophia* is here manifest not in glorious deeds or esoteric doctrine, but in God's solidarity with the one who suffers, which leads to life. Once the connection is made, the Pauline tradition goes on to speak freely of Jesus in wisdom categories. Like *Sophia* he is the one through whom all things were made (1 Cor 8:6); the image of the invisible God (Col 1:15); the firstborn of all creation (Col 1:15); the radiance of God's glory (Heb 1:3).[13]

In the synoptic gospels Jesus frequently appears as a sage, speaking words of wisdom in parables, beatitudes, maxims, proverbs and sayings. But he is more than that. Luke portrays him as a child of *Sophia* who communicates her gracious goodness by befriending the outcast (tax collectors and sinners) and who proves her right (justifies her) though he is rejected (7:35). Matthew goes further, putting *Sophia's* words in Jesus' mouth and having him do her deeds. Jesus calls to the heavy burdened to come to him, take on his yoke, and find rest—a precise Christological application of Wisdom's biblical words (Matt 11:28-30 from Sir 6:23-31). As does Wisdom, Jesus laments the rejection that people hand out to the prophets he sends them; he speaks a wisdom oracle depicting himself as a caring mother bird before withdrawing, like *Sophia*, from the city that rejects him (Matt 23:37-39). *Sophia's* intimate and exclusive knowledge of the ways of God shapes Jesus' words about knowing his Abba; like her, he reveals his intimate knowledge only to the little ones (Matt 11:25-27 from Wis 8:4). Matthew also equates "the deeds of the Christ" with Wisdom's deeds. Jesus' messianic acts of power enable people so that the blind see, the lame walk, the lepers are cleansed, the deaf hear, and the poor have the good news preached to them. These deeds draw withering scorn from this generation but, Matthew concludes, "Wisdom is vindicated by her deeds (11:2, 5, 19). In a nutshell, Matthew explicitly identifies Jesus with personified Wisdom herself.[14]

The fullest biblical flowering of wisdom Christology occurs in John's gospel, which is simply suffused with wisdom themes. Seeking and finding, feeding and nourishing, revealing and enlightening, giving life, making people friends of God, shining as light in the darkness, being the way, the truth, and the life: these are but some of the ways Jesus embodies *Sophia's* roles and is interpreted as Wisdom herself.

The prologue to this gospel, which more than any other scriptural text influences subsequent development in Christology, actually presents the pre-history of Jesus as the story of *Sophia*: present "in the beginning," an active agent in creation, a radiant light that darkness cannot overcome, descending from heaven to pitch a tent among the people, rejected by some, but giving life to those who seek (John 1:1-18). By most accounts, this prologue was originally an early Christian hymn to Wisdom which at its climax identifies her with Jesus the Christ.[15] Why the gospel's final redactor substituted the symbol of *Logos*/Word for *Sophia*/Wisdom in the hymn is a matter of some dispute. At least part of the reason lies with the gender issue as it became unseemly, given the developing patriarchal tendencies in the church, to interpret the male Jesus with a female symbol of God. As one male commentator observed, the fact that the *Logos* is masculine makes it a convenient substitute for "the awkward feminine figure."[16] Nevertheless, there is substantial scholarly agreement that in John's prologue the Word is a male surrogate for Wisdom whose story the prologue narrates in continuity with the wisdom tradition in the scriptures of Israel, where there is no such corresponding myth of the Word.

The use of wisdom categories to interpret Jesus had profound consequences. It enabled the fledgling Christian communities to attribute cosmic significance to the crucified Jesus, relating time to the creation and governance of the world. It deepened their understanding of his saving deeds by placing them in continuity with Wisdom's saving work throughout history. It was also the vehicle for developing insight into Jesus' ontological relationship with God. None of the other biblical symbols they used—Son of Man, Messiah, Son of God—connotes divinity in its original context, nor does the Word, which is barely personified in the Jewish scriptures. But Wisdom does. To identify the human being Jesus with divine *Sophia*, God's gracious nearness and activity in the world, moved thought to reflect that Jesus is not simply a human being inspired by God but must be related in a more personally unique way

to God. Jesus came to be seen as God's only-begotten Son
only after he was identified with Wisdom. Then her relation of intimacy with God was seen to be manifest in his
relation to God, her spirit seen in his, and his identity
shaped by hers. "Herein we see the origin of the doctrine
of incarnation,"[17] with consequences for trinitarian doctrine as well. Without the presence and strength of New
Testament sapiential Christology, insight into Jesus' identity and significance would have been very different indeed.

III. Jesus, the wisdom of God: untying the knot of sexist Christology

What does this rediscovery of wisdom offer for
speech about Jesus in women's voices in a community
struggling for the equal human dignity of women? First of
all, the wisdom tradition itself can widen the theological
playing field for discourse about Christ. Recall that the wisdom tradition is interested not only in God's mighty deeds
in history but in everyday life with the give and take of its
relationships. Recall too that wisdom is not under the control of the guardians of law or cult but is distilled from
reflection on experience. On both scores the door is open
for women, largely excluded from official religious circles,
to bring the trajectory of the wisdom tradition further by
reflecting on their own experience of the struggle and
beauty of everyday life, and naming this religiously important—every bit as significant as what occurs in more explicitly sacred times and places. In this manner new ways of
appreciating Christ can be born, less associated with patriarchal control and more in tune with women's daily life
and collective wisdom, so often discounted as a source of
insight. There is here an agenda yet to be carried out.
More specifically, the figure of personified Wisdom offers
an augmented field of female metaphors with which to

speak about Jesus the Christ in both his saving significance and his personal identity. And metaphors matter.

A. *Narrative.* The gospel can be proclaimed as the good news of this child and prophet of *Sophia*, sent to announce that she is a God of all-inclusive love who wills the wholeness and humanity of everyone, especially the poor and heavy burdened; sent to gather them all under the wings of their gracious *Sophia*-God and give them peace.[18] His parables, healings, exorcisms, and inclusive table community are Wisdom's deeds, revealing her renewing and friend-making power at work to establish the right order of creation. In his own pilgrimage through life he himself never ceased to be a seeker of wisdom, growing in knowledge of her ways through prayer, love, suffering, and his own life experience. Sometimes he calls her Abba; always he calls to those in the highways and the hedges to follow her path of life. Wisdom's gracious care is rejected as Jesus is executed, preeminent in a long line of her murdered prophets. Typically, her blessing of life finds him even in death and is given to him as a pledge of a future for all the dead. Her pure, mobile, people-loving Spirit is poured out upon the community of women and men gathered in his name, and they are charged to make her inclusive goodness experientially available to the ends of the earth.

B. *Doctrine.* Christological doctrine can also be expounded in wisdom categories. Here we are getting to the heart of the matter, for the metaphor "Son" and the relation between Father and Son have been the controlling categories of classical Christology. Releasing the symbol of Wisdom from subordination to Word or Son directs us to a different possibility. Whoever espouses a wisdom Christology is asserting that *Sophia* in all her fullness was in Jesus so that he manifests divine mystery in creative and saving involvement with the world. According to the doctrine of incarnation, Jesus is the human being *Sophia* became. It is interesting to discover that this way of speaking was common in the theology of the first Christian centuries. In the East, to cite but one example, Origen writes, "We believe...that God's Wisdom [*Sophia*] entered a woman's womb, was born as an infant, and wailed like crying children."[19] In the West Augustine, speaking first of the Spirit and then of Christ in relation to Wisdom/*Sapientia*, argues, "But she is sent in one way that she may be with human beings; and she has been sent in another way that she herself might be a human being."[20]

1. Jesus, the Wisdom of God: such a way of speaking breaks through the patriarchal assumption that there is a "necessary ontological connection"[21] between the male human being Jesus and a male God. The fluidity of gender symbolism in Jesus-*Sophia* breaks the stranglehold of androcentric thinking which fixates on the maleness of Jesus, the male metaphors of *Logos* and Son, and the relationship between Father and Son. This leads to the situation where gender is decentered, where it is not constitutive for the Christian doctrine of incarnation or for speech about Christ.

2. Jesus, the Wisdom of God: the male human being Jesus can be confessed to be revelatory of the graciousness of God symbolized as female. Likewise, Wisdom incarnate in Jesus addresses all persons with her call to be friends of God. Women as disciples of Jesus-*Sophia* share equally in the redemptive mission throughout time and can fully represent him. Not incidentally, the typical stereotypes of masculine and feminine are subverted as female *Sophia* represents creative transcendence, primordial passion for justice, and knowledge of the truth while Jesus expresses these divine characteristics in an immanent way relative to bodiliness and the earth. The creative, redeeming paradox of Jesus-*Sophia* points the way to a reconciliation of such

traditional opposites and their transformation from ene-
mies into a liberating, unified diversity.

3. Jesus, the Wisdom of God: such a symbol continues
to release the power of the good news inherent in the doctrine of incarnation and the proclamation of the resurrection of the crucified. If Wisdom herself became a human
being, then the very matter of creation in the flesh of
humanity belongs to her and is precious to her. There can
be no dichotomy between matter and spirit, or prizing of
one over the other, but matter itself is connected to God.
Resurrection announces that this will always be so, for it is
the body itself that is glorified in the power of her spirit,
rather than discarded. Furthermore, it is the tortured and
executed body of Jesus that is raised. This grounds
Christian hope for a future for all the dead, and explicitly
for all those who are tortured and unjustly destroyed in the
continuing torment of history. Wisdom's gift is ultimately
life.

4. Jesus, the Wisdom of God: this symbol is a crucially
helpful one in the ongoing struggle toward women's eman-
cipation in a community of genuine mutuality. Given the
intrinsic link between the patriarchal imagination in language and in structures, to liberate Christological language from a monopoly of male images and concepts is to
create a necessary, even if not sufficient, condition for further change in the church's consciousness and social order.
Furthermore, allowing the wisdom tradition to filter and
focus the significance of Jesus brings a whole range of values to bear that are dear to the hearts of feminist thinkers.
Friendship, connectedness, justice and prophecy, ecological care, delight and passion, suffering with, integrated
rather than dualistic patterns of relationship, the value of
the everyday in addition to the heroic deed, the value of
bodies as well as minds that seek the truth, the elusive
presence of God which is co-inherent with the world rather

than separated from and ruling over, right order that pervades everywhere: all of these enter into the interpretation of Jesus the Christ, setting doctrine off in a fundamentally new direction that coheres with the praxis of women's equal human dignity.

IV. Other ramifications

When personified wisdom is used as the interpretive symbol for Jesus the Christ she brings along, as we have seen, central ideas and themes of the wisdom tradition that also shape insight. In our day the answer to the question "Who do you say that I am?" is more importantly answered through praxis, through following the way of life, than through doctrinal formulations or theories. Interpretation of Christ is accomplished in the midst of conflict through the action of the community of disciples. Wisdom Christology done in the struggle for women's liberation also contributes to right behavior here in at least three major areas of current concern: justice for the poor, respectful encounter with world religions, and ecological care for the earth.

A. Justice in society is a central concern of the wisdom tradition of ancient Israel; it sees unjust conditions as a violation of the right order of creation. Yes, it is a tradition that prizes wealth and riches—but not at the expense of the neighbor. According to Proverbs, "Those who oppress the poor insult their Maker," while those who reach out to the poor honor God (14:31). Accordingly, the wisdom literature is replete with advice on caring for the widow and orphan and the poor man; with warning that those who are greedy for gain will be caught in their own snare; and with instruction to rulers to love righteousness and govern accordingly: "The righteous know the rights of the poor; the wicked have no such understanding" (Prov

29:7). There is potential in the wisdom tradition for political critique of injustice.

Personified Wisdom herself betrays a strong identification with the concerns of justice. "I walk," she says, "in the way of righteousness, along the paths of justice" (Prov 8:20). Her principles affect not only personal interactions but the social-political order as well: "By me kings reign, and rulers decree what is just; by me rulers rule, and nobles, all who govern rightly" (Prov 8:15-16). In an act that has become paradigmatic for all liberation, Wisdom leads her people out from a nation of oppressors, becoming to them a starry flame of guidance until they find a safe home (Wis 10:15-19).

Interpreting the historical ministry and death of Jesus, his own option for the poor and the price he paid for it, in the context of the wisdom tradition shows that the passion of God is clearly directed toward the lifting of social oppression and the establishing of right relations. The table is set for those who will come, the bread and wine ready to nourish the struggle. What is needed is to listen to the loud cries of Jesus-*Sophia* resounding in the cries of the poor, violated, and desperate, and to ally our lives as the wisdom community to the divine creative, redeeming work of establishing right order in the world.[22]

B. There is a universal, non-exclusive character to the wisdom tradition that coheres with today's recognition of value in all of the world's religions. The sages tend to talk not so much about the "God of Israel" or the "God of our fathers" as about the Creator of all, present and moving everywhere. Again, righteousness and insight are not confined to those of the Jewish faith; even Job was not an Israelite.

Personified Wisdom herself symbolizes God's presence and activity throughout the whole world, not just in Israel. In her grand tour of the world she describes how she holds sway over every people and nation; in every one she has gotten a possession (Sir 24:6). Her kindly, people-loving spirit fills the world, pervading everything and holding all things together (Wis 1:6-7). Her light shines against the darkness everywhere, and those whom she makes to be friends of God and prophets are found in every nation.

Interpreting the meaning of Jesus in this context highlights the universalism inherent in his life, ministry, and destiny. Jesus-*Sophia* personally incarnates Wisdom's gracious care in one particular history, for the benefit of all, while she lays down a multiplicity of paths in diverse cultures by which all people may seek, and seeking find her. There is then a continuity of divine action and inspiration between the Christian religion and the multitude of world religious traditions. Jesus uniquely focuses Wisdom for Christians, but the same reality is focused differently in other religious traditions. Wisdom discourse thus directs the community toward a global, ecumenical perspective respectful of other religious faiths.[23]

C. A relation to the whole cosmos is already built into the biblical wisdom tradition. Its interest lies in the right order of creation and it focuses often and intensely on human life in the context of an interrelated natural world, both ideally forming a harmonious whole. When wisdom is given to Solomon he is enabled:

> to know the structure of the world and the activity of the elements, the beginning and middle and end of times, the alternations of the solstices and the changes of the seasons, the cycles of the year and the constellations of the stars, the natures of animals and the tempers of wild animals, the powers of wind and the thoughts of human beings, the varieties of plants and the

virtues of roots: I learned both what is secret and what is manifest, for wisdom, the fashioner of all things, taught me (Wis 7:17-22).

Personified Wisdom is the mother of all these good things (Wis 7:12), or the master craftswoman through whom they were all made (Prov 8:30). Reaching mightily from one end of the earth to the other she orders all things well, and delights in them (!), playing in the world with rejoicing and elusive gaiety.

Interpreting the ministry, death and resurrection of Jesus by means of the wisdom tradition orients Christology beyond the human world to the ecology of the earth and, indeed, to the universe, a vital move in this era of planetary crisis. As the embodiment of *Sophia* who is fashioner of all that exists, Jesus' redeeming care extends to the flourishing of all creatures and the whole earth itself. The power of Wisdom's spirit is evident wherever human beings share in this love for the earth, tending its fruitfulness, respecting its limits, restoring what has been damaged, and guarding it from destruction. In this spirit the community of Jesus-*Sophia* finds its mandate to be in solidarity with the earth and at the forefront of ecological care.[24]

Conclusion

The wisdom tradition as a whole with its symbol of personified female Wisdom and its sapiential Christology is a largely untapped resource for speaking about Jesus Christ. If we connect it, critically, with women's experience, and read it with a liberation hermeneutic, what emerges is a beneficial field of metaphors, concepts, and values with which to articulate the meaning of Christ and ourselves as a community of equal disciples. The struggle toward such a community both in the church and society is enormous. There is backlash, fierce opposition, fear, and consequently much discouragement. Those who love Wisdom need to go on singing the old Advent hymn, drawing strength from her spirit moving everywhere to order all things rightly. May she teach us in her ways to go.

Notes

For detailed background on Wisdom see Elizabeth Johnson, "Jesus, the Wisdom of God: A Biblical Basis for a Non-Androcentric Christology," *Ephemerides Theologiae Louvaniensis* 61(1985): 261-94.

1. For surveys of the scholarly literature see Ulrich Wilckens, "Sophia," *Theological Dictionary of the New Testament* 7:465-528; R.B. Scott, "The Study of the Wisdom Literature," *Interpretation* 24(1970): 20-45; Roland Murphy, *The Tree of Life: An Exploration of Biblical Wisdom Literature–Anchor Bible Reference Library* (NY: Doubleday, 1990).

2. See Carole Fontaine, "The Personification of Wisdom," in *Harper's Bible Commentary* (San Francisco: Harper and Row, 1988), 501-503. For the goddess behind Sophia, Canaanite and Semitic sources are supported by William Albright, "The Goddess of Life and Wisdom," *American Journal of Semitic Languages and Literature* 36(1919/20): 258-94; the Egyptian Maat is explored by Christa Kayatz, *Studien zu Proverbien* 1-9(Neukirchen-Vluyn: Neukirchener Verlag, 1966). Advocates of Isis include Wilfred Know, "The Divine Wisdom," *Journal of Theological Studies* 38(1937): 230-37; Hans Conzelmann, "The Mother of Wisdom," in *The Future of Our Religious Past,* ed. James Robinson (NY: Harper & Row, 1971), 230-43; and John Kloppenborg, "Isis and Sophia in the Book of Wisdom," *Harvard Theological Review* 75(1982): 57-84, a study important for its methodological observations.

3. Gerhard von Rad, *Wisdom in Israel* (Nashville: Abingdon, 1972).

4. Berhard Lang, *Wisdom and the Book of Proverbs: An Israelite Goddess Redefined* (NY: Pilgrim, 1986).

5. R.N. Whybray, *Wisdom in Proverbs: The Concept of Wisdom in Proverbs* 1-9 (Naperville, IL: A.R. Allenson, 1965).

6. Helmer Ringgren, *Word and Wisdom: Studies in the Hypostatization of Divine Qualities and Functions in the Ancient Near East* (Lund: H. Ohlssons, 1947).

7. Roland Murphy, *Seven Books of Wisdom* (Milwaukee: Bruce, 1960), 11, 143; C. Larcher, *Études sur le livre de la Sagesse* (Paris: J. Gabalda, 1969), 402-14; Elisabeth Schüssler-Fiorenza, *In Memory of Her: A Feminist Theological Reconstruction of Christian Origins* (NY: Crossroad, 1983), 133.

8. James Dunn's argument, "Was Christianity a Monotheistic Faith from the Beginning?" *Scottish Journal of Theology* 35 (1982): 319-20.

9. Ludwig Blau, "Shekinah," *The Jewish Encyclopedia* (NY: Funk and Wagnalls, 1905) 11:258-60; Dale Moody, "Shekinah," *Interpreters Dictionary of the Bible* 4 (Nashville: Abingdon, 1962): 317-19.

10. For the synthetic character of late wisdom, see Harmut Gese, "Wisdom, Son of Man, and the Origins of Christology: The Consistent Development of Biblical Theology," *Horizons in Biblical Theology* 3(1981): 23-57.

11. See James Dunn, *Christology in the Making* (Philadelphia: Westminster, 1980), 163-212.

12. Hans Conzelmann, "Paul und die Weisheit," *New Testament Studies* 12(1965/66): 231-44; Martin Hengel, *Judaism and Hellenism* 1 (London: SCM, 1973), 157-62; and James Davies, *Wisdom and Spirit: An Investigation of 1 Cor.* 1:18-3:20 *Against the Background of Jewish Sapiential Traditions in the Greco-Roman Period* (Lanham, MD: University Press of America, 1984).

13. Elisabeth Schüssler-Fiorenza, "Wisdom Mythology and the Christological Hymns of the New Testament," in *Aspects of Wisdom in Judaism and Early Christianity,* ed. Robert Wilkens (Notre Dame, IN: University of Notre Dame Press, 1975), 17-41.

14. James Robinson, "Jesus as Sophos and Sophia: Wisdom Tradition and the Gospels," in *Aspects of Wisdom,* 1-16; M. Jack

Suggs, *Christology and Law in Matthew's Gospel* (Cambridge, MA: Harvard University Press, 1970); who is disputed by Marshall Johnson, "Reflections on a Wisdom Approach in Matthew's Christology," *Catholic Biblical Quarterly* 36(1974): 44-64; and Celia Deutsch, "Wisdom in Matthew: Transformation of a Symbol," *Novum Testamentum* 32(1990): 13-47.

15. Rendel Harris, "The Origin of the Prologue to St. John's Gospel," *The Expositor* 12(1916): 147-70; 314-20; 388-400; 415-26; Raymond Brown, *The Gospel According to John, I-XII* (Garden City, NY: Doubleday, 1966), cxxii-cxxviii, 3-37, 519-24; John Ashton, "The Transformation of Wisdom: A Study of the Prologue of John's Gospel," *New Testament Studies* 32(1986): 161-86.

16. Wilfred Knox, *Paul and the Church of the Gentiles* (Cambridge: Cambridge University Press, 1934), 84. Most men authors make a passing reference to this reason but do not analyze it; e.g., R. Barbour, "Creation, Wisdom and Christ," *Creation, Christ and Culture,* ed. Richard McKinney (Edinburgh: T & T Clark, 1976), 38. But see Joan Chamberlain Engelsman, *The Feminine Dimension of the Divine* (Philadelphia: Westminster, 1979), 74-120.

17. Dunn, *Christology in the Making,* 212.

18. See Schüssler-Fiorenza, *In Memory of Her,* 130-40.

19. Origen, De princ. 2:6.2. For overviews of the use of wisdom in this period see H. Jaeger, "The Patristic Conception of Wisdom in the Light of Biblical and Rabbinical Research," *Studia Patristica,* ed. F. Cross (Berlin: Akademie Verlag, 1961) 4:90-106; Robert Grant, "The Book of Wisdom at Alexandria," *After the New Testament* (Philadelphia: Fortress, 1967), 70-82.

20. *Sapientia*: "Sed aliter mittitur ut sit cum homine; aliter missa est ut ipsa sit homo."—Augustine, De Trin 4:20, 27; *Nicene and Post-Nicene Fathers* Vol. 3, ed. Philip Schaff (Grand Rapids, MI: Eerdmans, 1956).

21. Rosemary Radford Ruether, *Sexism and God-Talk: Toward a Feminist Theology* (Boston: Beacon, 1983), 117.

22. Bruce Malchow, "Social Justice in the Wisdom Literature," *Biblical Theology Bulletin* 12(1982): 120-24; Leo

Lefebure, *Toward a Contemporary Wisdom Christology: A Study of Karl Rahner and Norman Pittenger* (Lanham, MD: University Press of America, 1988), 199-222.

23. R.S. Sugirtharajah, "Wisdom, Q, and a Proposal for a Christology," *Expository Times* 102 no. 2 (Nov. 1990): 42-46.

24. Roland Murphy, "Wisdom and Creation," *Journal of Biblical Literature* 104(1985): 3-11; Loren Wilkinson, "Cosmic Christology and the Christian's Role in Creation," *Christian Scholar's Review* 11(1981): 18-40.

Feminist Christologies: Re-Dressing the Tradition[1]

ELEANOR McLAUGHLIN

The most pleased of the lot was the other lion, who kept running about everywhere pretending to be very busy but really in order to say to everyone he met. "Did you hear what he said? 'Us lions.' That means him and me. 'Us lions.'"[2]

The Holy Scriptures and theological tradition are clear that the Deity transcends human sexuality, but they also accord a privileged status, interpreted through the Cross, to the masculine metaphors and terms of address.[3]

Setting the problem

Women yearn for the experience of the newly freed lions of Narnia, to hear the icon of God say "Us women." The gender of the Son of God as a Christological problem is a relatively new question and a strongly controverted one, even among feminists.[4] In the ordinary practice and preaching of the churches, the assumption remains strong, especially in the liberal churches, that there is no problem for women in traditional Christology or the language of worship because Jesus, though a man, saves by virtue of "his" humanity. During debate among Episcopalians over the ordination of women, Richard Norris argued forcefully against those who did not believe it possible for women to be priests by asserting that the maleness of Jesus symbolized no important theological principle.[5] John Macquarrie's recent survey of the history of Christological doctrine makes no mention at all of the gender issues raised by feminists, dismissing the soteriological significance of Jesus' maleness in one brief aside. "Sexuality is an essential constitutive element in every human being, and Jesus was a man in the secondary sense that he was of the male sex. But I do not think there is any theological importance to this. Being human was essential to Jesus as the Christ; being male was, as far as I can see, contingent."[6]

In contrast to the liberal dismissal of Jesus' gender as a theological issue, the more conservative churches understand the maleness of Jesus as a necessary symbol of the very essence of the Christian God and Gospel. Grounded in an essentialist understanding of both human sexuality and the realist symbolic character of God-language and ritual, the Anglican theologian, E.L. Mascall argues: "...the maleness of Jesus cannot be separated from the masculine imagery of revelation. He is the express image of the Father." Hence, he continues: "...the priesthood of Christ is...in some profound and mysterious sense that lies behind and provides the ground of the biological differentiation, a male function."[7] Indeed, that the being and ministry of Jesus Christ relate in some real way to sexual differentiation is celebrated each time the Marriage Office from the Book of Common Prayer is read:

> ...our Lord Jesus Christ adorned this manner of life by his presence and first miracle at a wedding in Cana of Galilee. It signifies to us the

mystery of the union between Christ and his
Church...[8]

Jesus Christ is the Bridegroom, an image not only gen-
dered, but sexual. As a much quoted United States layman
Thomas Howard, a recent pilgrim from Canterbury to
Rome, puts it:

> Jews and Christians worship the God who has
> gone to vast and prolonged pains to disclose
> himself to us as he not she, as King and not
> Queen, and for Christians as Father not Mother,
> and who sent his Son not his daughter in his
> final unveiling of himself for our eyes.[9]

It is not only conservatives, but most women in the
pew who join academic theologians in an impatient rejection of the feminist complaint that women cannot find a
"savior" in this God-Man Jesus, so shaped are we all by the
teaching that Jesus Christ is the Representative Man (sic),
the Second Adam, the Man for Others, *Ecce Homo*, and
therefore beyond or inclusive of all sexuality. It is therefore
difficult to get this conversation about the gender of Jesus
going within a culture which generally does not recognize
that "generic humanity" has, at least since Aristotle, been
constructed normatively male, including women only as
"defective and misbegotten." Our historicized mind-set
cannot imagine an alternative to the "obvious" maleness of
the Jesus of Nazareth; our devotions celebrate this maleness as we sing, "Unto us a Boy is born, to us a Son is
given...," and whether believer or secular post-modern, we
intuitively reject any alternative. We see evidence of this
unconscious anger in the public revulsion which greeted
Edwina Sandy's sculpture exhibited at the Cathedral of St.
John the Divine, "Christa," an icon of Jesus as Crucified

Woman. Resistance to any modification of the male imaging of Jesus and God can be read in the continued discomfort and, in some quarters, hostility to women exercising priesthood in the Episcopal Church and the rejection of women in priesthood by the majority of Anglican, Orthodox and Roman Catholic Christians the world over.

The problem I wish to address lies in the unsatisfactory responses of liberal or conservative approaches to the problems for feminist women inherent in the male gender of the incarnate God. The liberal solution, that Jesus' maleness is secondary to his humanity, of no theological or soteriological significance, insofar as representative man is believed to include all of humankind, is no solution for many women. This liberal argument is unacceptable because it is dishonest. In fact, the cultural symbols of maleness and "generic" humanity have never included women without qualification, and certainly do not do so in our contemporary United States culture. The conservative argument, that the maleness of Jesus is crucial to the classical Christian theological tradition, may be more honest and accurate to the ways in which that tradition has been interpreted and commonly understood until very recently. Therefore, if there is to be found or constructed a feminist Christology which includes woman as well as man in the icon of God, the male hegemony must be deconstructed such that the image of God made Flesh is seen and experienced as female as well as male. We need a Jesus as "like me," a woman, in such a way that as we look at him in prayer and praise, there can be an experience like to that of the freed lion of Narnia, hearing Aslan call "us lions." We need a Jesus as God/man and stranger who is also God/woman, friend, sister, mother;..."like unto us in all things, excepting sin."

An alternative feminist Christology: reclaiming the body

Before arguing for this re-visioned Christology, I will suggest some of the ways in which I differ from, or would modify some of the principal contemporary feminist Christologies. In the course of this ground laying, the components will emerge which I find necessary for a Christology in which women find themselves subjects in God's image, whole and holy.

I would begin with some basic postulates such as those set forth by the Anglican theologian, John Macquarrie. He points to the two authoritative sources for knowledge of Jesus Christ, "...testimony of the past and experience of the present."[10] Furthermore, he argues that "...the significance of Jesus Christ was not seen all at once," and that who Jesus was is inseparable from who Jesus is in the Christ-Event of the church's response in faith. Jesus Christ is the Word preached.[11] And I would add, Jesus Christ is the sacraments celebrated and the Christian life lived. Macquarrie affirms that Jesus Christ is both historical fact and trans-historical symbol,[12] and the Christological titles are thus not limited to a particular culture, even that of the writers of the New Testament texts.[13] It would seem that this mainstream theologian presses for a Jesus Christ who is not the same today as yesterday. Thus, Macquarrie searches for modifications of the tradition similar to those proposed by many feminist Christians, though he, in his otherwise exhaustive book, strangely ignores gender questions. I also seek a Christology adequate to contemporary experience and therefore responsive to the feminist difficulties with Jesus' maleness, and like Macquarrie, I seek a revisionist Christology recognizably connected to the tradition, if that is possible. In particular, I look for a Christ symbol not only intellectually adequate but also with which women and men can worship. A "usable" Christology must be "prayable," for I am convinced that human beings were made to worship.

Macquarrie, citing James Dunn, offers an "...irreducible minimum without which Christianity loses any distinctive definition,"[14] which involves affirmation of the historical Jew Jesus, presumably fully (but not ordinarily) human, experienced as an exalted being, agent of God, supreme Lord, Son of God. This is a high Christology, to which I do not hold our discussants, for unlike Hampson,[15] I am unwilling to put out of the conversation about Jesus, people who don't fit any one or a dozen definitions of "really Christian." I am willing to play on a field without foul lines—it enriches the conversation. So I would not omit from the discussion positions which might be considered inadequately "Christian," even those who seek in the goddess an alternative to the incarnation. The history of Christian heresy reveals that the most creative discourse is that which contains the widest number of options. Justin Martyr claimed that all which is human, is of Christ.

With Carter Heyward, who identified herself as "hooked on Jesus,"[16] this Jesus-narrative, and the symbols which ritualize the narrative seem central not only to me but also to Western culture. For that reason, I am not attracted to move outside the Christ-Event and the biblical narratives as the foundational paradigms in which the self and the holy are sought. Despite the unquestioned spiritual creativity which has been let loose by the rediscovery of the various ancient goddess religions, I have some serious difficulties with this alternative to a re-visioned Christology. For women, a historical sacred narrative does better than a mythological one, as it presents the opportunity to deal with embodiment as an aspect of the sacred. Another problem presented by goddess spirituality is the ease with which it commits the sin which it purports to address, the exclusion of one half of the human race from an immediate experience of the holy as other and like. We need all forms of creation to be found in God, the "chalice and the blade." A third problem for feminists raised by goddess spirituality lies in the realm of the ethical. I have yet to see the goddess rites so understood and celebrated as to form up a sense of "right" and "good" by which daily choice may be made and human institutions shaped. I miss in the goddess spiritualities a well worked out understanding of sin and its remedy. There is also the fundamental problem, that the goddesses, not unlike Mary, may be as fully a product of patriarchy as their consorts and sons. Finally, to create cult and theology from scratch, with so few extant texts and traditions, seems more difficult than working with a fully fledged religious tradition which shapes our culture and unconscious even more dangerously if we ignore it. These caveats notwithstanding, the goddesses stand to correct, to supplant, to nurture, to give birth to much new life in the Christological debates among feminists. The place of the erotic in the Holy and the encounter of the Holy in our bodied experiences of loving, feeding, birthing, desiring, and ecstatic consummating union are urgent questions which goddess spirituality helps us to address. The crying need for a Christology which embraces earth and all earth creatures could also be the result of these conversations between theology and Christology.

An aspect of many feminist Christologies, for example the work of Daphne Hampson, is a certain unexamined commitment to Enlightenment epistemologies.[17] I do not, for example, believe that the heart of the feminist theological enterprise is the achievement of equality between men and women.[18] Too often equality in our culture means a black or Hispanic man or woman, or dominant culture woman entering the social system under the ground rules of the white male tradition. The admittedly dangerous invitation to explore what woman made in God's image might mean on women's terms suggests that equality is but one among many values. The discovery of woman-self, woman-voice and woman-in-relation as woman made in God's image, must take priority over, even stand in criticism of, a male-defined autonomous subjectivity or a spurious equality which defines woman in terms of male constructions of the human.

Many feminist Christian women ground their Christologies implicitly on Galatians 3:28, that eschatological vision of the baptized community where "...there is neither Jew nor Greek, there is neither slave nor free, there is neither male nor female, for you are all one in Christ Jesus." Following the ground-breaking work of Elaine Pagels, many search for a way of being beyond sexuality in the extra-canonical gnostic texts where androgynous spiritualities beyond sexual dualism seem to offer attractive models for re-formed, non-hierarchical Christian community.[19] Indeed, there are many analogies between some feminist, New Age spiritualities and the gnostic sensibilities of the early Christian centuries. This is not a direction which I find useful. It was and remains, predominantly anti-incarnational, anti-body, dualist, anti-sensual and profoundly individualistic. The gnostic journey is personal, and does not ground a spirituality for community. The gnostic Christ has no body. That is too easy a way to be rid of the phallic-signifier.

Many feminist Christologies share the strong bias of the liberal Protestant theological tradition which, since Schleiermacher, has sought to dismantle high Christological dogma in favor of a renewed sense of the full humanity of Jesus.[20] Such Christology "from below" has the advantage of taking seriously the New Testament narratives, full of Jesus as healer, liberator, friend of sinners, outcasts, and women. Combined with the history of religions, this preference for the historical Jesus can question the claims of Christianity to a unique revelation of God in Jesus Christ and thus enable mutually enriching conversations with other religious communities. A Christology from below also accords with the feminist call for the priority of experience over extrinsic authority as the place of meeting with the Holy. Additionally, the tendency to "let go" of preexistence, miracles, up to and not excluding the resurrection, and other instances of the affirmation of providential interruptions of natural causality occasions less dissonance with modern, Enlightenment models of reality. As will be evident, I am willing to be anti-Enlightenment and entertain a "second naiveté" in the presence of this powerful religious symbol, Jesus Christ. Without denying that Jesus of Nazareth is a real human historical figure, I affirm that the symbol reality of Jesus, which carries the specifically religious experience of the holy, is as important to me as what little the historians can say about that "heretical Jew, Jesus." What we know about religious experience is learned and spoken of symbolically. And of Jesus there is no history free of the interpretation of religious symbol...whether in words or ritual gestures, song or sculpture or sacred building. These interpretive symbols, never wholly loosed from history, may be played with. That is the game theologians play. It is up to the community to set the rules and the playing field in this entertainment of symbols which is more a dance than a game. This is not a new move. Macquarrie reminds us that the "life of Jesus has not more reality than the abstractions of Byzantine theology or the Pantocrator staring at us from the midst of a dazzling mosaic."[21] The only novelty in my approach may be my insistence on the God-ness of Jesus Christ while seeking to uncover through his Sacred Humanity the lost Woman-God. I do believe, that without the God-ness there is no way to deconstruct, un-center, uncover the male-ness so that the woman-ness of God/Jesus can be seen and shared. If Jesus is not something more than a first century Jewish rabbi, this enterprise is more trouble than it is worth.

The historical particularity may not be lost from a feminist Christology, as so often happens when, with relief, women leave the male Jesus of childhood piety for the Christ of mature theological reflection.[22] Origen played that intellectually elitist game also, leaving the Jesus healer and savior for the unsophisticated whilst the spiritual "knower" could look to union with the Logos. Here our African American sisters are extraordinarily helpful, as they witness to the power of the historical Jesus. Jesus the liberator, who in his particularity is black, stands with and redeems the particularity of black suffering.[23] It is significant for this feminist enterprise that the discussion of or depiction of a black or Chinese Jesus has caused no particular outcry. James Cone and womanist theologians like Jacquelyn Grant have been able successfully to contend for a Jesus who though male is experienced as black. This stands in sharp contrast to the outrage which greeted "Christa," the sculpture of Jesus, the woman crucified. The icon was described by opponents as "reprehensible and desecrating...totally changing the symbol."[24] This response is a reminder of the power of body, and of Jesus' historically particular male body. At last, with the new culturally presented opportunity to inscribe the Word made flesh in a black body or a woman's body, we can once again feel the power of the first century scandal and stumbling block which was Jesus in that/our world. For first century Jews and Greeks, God in any body was a scandal, a "clothing" of the universal in the particular and vice versa. A feminist Christology must seek just such embodiment,

female embodiment, with all the outrage and erotic energies which that *kenosis* of male privilege arouses.

In keeping with the Enlightenment and the liberal
roots of the women's movement, too many feminist
Christologies have simply avoided all such body-talk with
its sexual penumbra. For instance, Suchocki's process
Christology laments the reduction of "God" to maleness in
the face of the Old Testament portrayal of a god beyond
sexuality...and she would keep this godly absence of
"...strictly human features."[25] Such an approach does not
meet the demands of women (and many men). The desic-
cating dualisms of traditional Christianity and indeed of
all Western discourse must be dismantled so that the
sacred might once again be found in all embodied experience of life. These Christological reflections, by locating in
the Incarnate God the place where the creator/creature
dualism is shattered, also propose a violation of the gender dualism, male/female. Such a breaking of the boundaries opens to us a re-vision of the holy in which relational-
ity, sexuality, feeling and the feminine join mind and word
at the center of our God symbols. Carter Heyward has
written most powerfully of this need.[26] A re-visioned
Christology must recover the unitive energies of the erotic.
Such a spirituality of desire was known to the mystics from
Plato's myth of yearning wholeness in the *Symposium,* from
St. Bernard's confidence that in the desiring is the tasting
of God, and from the impassioned union of the mystical
marriage of the soul with Jesus. Whether the eros of
Brautmystik or the spiritual birth-giving by which the
Christian is "pregnant" with God as Holy Child within (cel-
ebrated by Meister Eckhart, Catherine of Siena, and
Birgitta of Sweden) these embodied devotions of late
medieval mystical piety represent an experience of Jesus as
mother, wife, sister, lover, and infant beneath our hearts.[27]
It is to this tradition of embodied spirituality that we look

to overcome the body-fearing interpretations of the New Testament texts on God's love and friendship.

Feminist Christologies have been caught up in the questions of Chalcedon, arguing a fourth century dilemma about how to reconcile within the metaphysics of a dualist late-Platonic and Stoic world view, the apparent paradox of a human being, experienced as God.[28] In contrast to this consciousness of the fourth century, it is not divinity/humanity, but the male/female dualism which bedevils the cultural place in which we stand. Therefore, we have to argue what seems apparently as nonsensical as the Chalcedonian paradox of full divinity and full humanity in one person. How is Jesus Christ a person whom we can experience as either man or woman? This discourse may not be carried out principally in word symbols, as was the case with our inheritance of the fourth century debates. Rather, we may need ritual and visual symbols as well as words. Only thus can this be a Christology, a way of imaging Jesus Christ, which can be prayed and ritualized by the people of God. Evagrius Ponticus, from a fourth century desert, reminds us that the theologian is ". . . one whose prayer is true."[29] Without further description of my task, let me begin it.

Some pieces of the body of Christ, treasures old and new

What follows is not a complete Christology. Indeed, here I offer a suggestion of possible hermeneutical moves, or new paradigms, and point to some places in the Western Christian tradition where one might look to find conversation partners for the exploration of the religious questions raised by the contemporary experiences of women (and some men). I write as one still confident that the gospel accounts of Jesus are primal and life giving story. With Judy Chicago I must affirm, "Our heritage is our power."[30]

We have seen and acknowledged the serious problem for many contemporary Christians which resides in the seemingly indisputable historical "fact" that Jesus of Nazareth, who is worshiped as Christ and Lord, is/was a real male person. Further this male Christ, symbolized religiously, has been used to subordinate, to dehumanize, and to render women invisible and voiceless. Feminist Christologies maneuver to avoid this "fact," notably with a Bultmannian existentialist and de-mythologizing focus on the "Christ-event" of contemporary experience. For the reasons above, I argue that feminist Christology may not so lightly dismiss the "body." Without returning to a "primal naiveté" of a pre-modern consciousness, I propose we remythologize and resymbolize, with the help of the pre-Reformation spiritual tradition, to discover a Jesus who is for humanity, very God, very man, and very woman, or perhaps never simply God or only man. This reconstruction of God-Symbol is essential if Christianity is to break through androcentrism to the Gospel. It will have a destabilizing impact on the culture at large, by de-authorizing the traditional Christologies which have been so limiting and demeaning of women, Jews, African-Americans, and others who do not fall within the "norms" of white, male Western Christian civilization. The feminist requirement that women be genuinely included in Jesus' humanity could be seen as a faithful response to the evangelical promise, "God so loved the world..." not merely as an exercise in "secular humanism" or modernist heresy. The way I have made this discovery about Jesus Christ flows out of experience, through the tradition, to a literary-critical paradigm shift and back into experience.

The experience with which I begin is my own, from childhood, a dimly heard call to be an Anglican priest. The tradition is that now widely seen and appreciated strain of pre-Reformation piety through which Jesus (and sometimes God, Father and Spirit) is addressed, prayed to, and sacramentally experienced as woman, true body (and woman culturally represents body),[31] also as lover, child, and nursing infant. The literary critical paradigm is that of the transvestite, the taboo, transgressive, Third One who dismantles the dualisms, male/female, law/gospel, insider/outsider, friend/enemy, God/world. And finally, the returning experience is the history of women priests in the United States Episcopal Church, whose being as God-persons and ways of presiding and ministering are deconstructing androcentric images and theologies. We are changing, as opponents promised we would, the ways in which God/Jesus/woman-self are experienced. We are bursting out of the categories and truly changing the gods.

The experience

As the Episcopal Church, led by the "secular" women's movement of the late 1960s and 1970s, began to consider the possibility that women could be called to Holy Orders by God and by the community, this cradle Episcopalian, then a young professor of medieval history at Wellesley College, began to feel long repressed stirrings. I could not, however, imagine a woman priest, for there were no words or icons which gave permission to see that new thing under the sun. It was my Harvard thesis advisor, who knew me and my searchings, who told me of an obscure French scholarly article titled "A Little Known Medieval Devotion to Jesus Our Mother."[32] The first article in English on this topic was thus written out of my personal dilemma, the tension between my sense of myself as a woman and a call to priesthood. I understood priesthood quite traditionally and, with psychological accuracy, I

understood it as an office in which one stood, symbolically, *in persona Christi*.[33] To discover, therefore, that Jesus can
be prayed to as a woman and represented by a woman,
indeed as a mother like me, was an empowerment to
action on behalf of structural and theological change in
the Church and a recognition of my own vocation. I
argued for the priesthood of women not in the liberal or
Enlightenment language of "rights" but rather as a matter
of theology—can Jesus Christ be represented by a woman-
priest, does Jesus represent women? Can I, woman, made
in God's image, see myself in God incarnate, and speak
with the authoritative subjectivity of the New Adam, naming the world and offering with Christ the sacrifice of
praise and thanksgiving?

The tradition

The address to Jesus as a woman, primarily, as mother, begins early in the tradition and becomes more fre-
quent from the twelfth century onward as devotion to the
Sacred Humanity of Jesus and his mother flourishes.[34] The
only gospel mother-naming, the synoptic mother-hen
metaphor, is a self referent, significantly in the context of
recalling Jerusalem's history of "...killing the prophets and
stoning those who are sent to you. How often would I have
gathered your children together as a hen gathers her
brood under her wings, and you would not!" (Matthew
23:37). This language may not be dismissed as mere literary trope, for the apophatic tradition reminds us that
Christianity's "...sacred texts are chronicles of experience,
armories of metaphor, and purveyors of an interpretive
tradition."[35] No longer may we give authority to naive distinctions between metaphysical or even "historical" propo-
sitions about God contrasted to the language of prayer or
poetry, as if the propositional language of the theologian

or the evidence of the historical method told the truth about the really real more surely than the figurative and affective language of the poet. A rediscovery of the truth-telling status of metaphorical language, known by the pre-scholastics, is part of the methodology of the renewed theology Christian feminists seek.

Female Jesus-naming throughout the tradition comes up as the bearer of particular theological motifs and in the literature of devotion rather than that of "school" theology. Clement of Alexandria, writing of Christ the Educator, experiences in both God the Father and Jesus *Logos*, "care-banishing breasts" affording "...the milk of love given by the Word who is father and mother, teacher and nurse."[36] The nurture and teaching of the embodied *Logos* known in the human Jesus, church, and sacraments, contrast to the spiritualizing flight from embodiment of the gnostics whom Clement opposed. When spiritualizing threatens to "erase" the reality of Incarnation, Jesus is seen woman-wise. Hence the devotion and defense of Mary, *Theotokos*, to face down docetism. To recover the female face of God is to be faithful to Catholic Christianity.

Carolyn Bynum shows how twelfth century Cistercian abbots, anxious about the tensions raised between the Gospel imperative of maternal charity and the good order of legal structures in their exercise of authority, used female namings for God and Jesus and themselves as abbots and mothers to their monastic charges.[37] St. Anselm, reflecting with theological rigor upon the incarnation and the atonement, shaped not only by feudal theories of harsh justice and honor but also by the early death of his mother and his own struggles for survival with an unyielding king, prayed, "Great Lord our elder brother seated next to Great Lady, our best of mothers,"[38] rule and mercy one. Could his address to "Christ, my mother" whose gentleness comforts the frightened, and sweet smell revives the despairing...from whom flows consolation, and whose "... warmth gives life to the dead,"[39] be the female body of community which nurtures and saves, even though clothed in the maleness, which rules. The text, "Therefore you are fathers by your effect/and mothers by your affection"[40] referring here to both St. Paul and Jesus, as it assumes and affirms sexual stereotypes, also challenges the world's images. Paul and Jesus are seen as women in this transgressive text which breaks the categories with mother/man language. Not androgyny, each is each, fully; Jesus and Paul are mothers and men.

The now familiar Revelations of Dame Julian of Norwich, whose Mother Jesus naming is most theologically contextualized, can also be read as texts of dis-closure. This "gendered" Jesus, i.e. Jesus as woman, is no "add-on" or gesture of Jungian complementarity, or androgynous non-person. Rather, this is a topsy-turvy and upsetting text with its litany of "Mother Jesus, He." Categories and boundaries are sundered as the whole universe is seen in a hazelnut, all the while no anger is seen in God.[41] This is in the face of the church's clear teaching upon the reality of divine judgment and her own experience of the pain of sin. But Julian never allows herself to "fall" into the categories heretic or orthodox. She sits in her anchorhold, cloistered and alone, yet in sight of the bustle of Norwich, writing private visions for the sake of a Christian public, every simple Evenchristian. From the single broken body of this Man/Mother streams the water and blood which gives birth to and nourishes community, Mother Church. Even more astounding, "...our beloved Mother, Jesus, feeds us with himself...."[42] The terrible pain and outward, physical sight of crucifixion is Julian's joy and spiritual insight. She saw physically, "in actual vision, in imaginative understanding, and in spiritual sight."[43] The intertwining of inside and outside, of physical and spiritual, both/and, not either/or, is, I am suggesting, represented by Jesus' Motherhood, always coupled with the male pronoun. "And of his goodness he opens the eye of our understanding so that we can see."[44] The meaning of these "shewings" she sums up in the last chapter: "You would know our Lord's meaning in this thing? Know it well. Love was his meaning. Who showed it to you? Love. What did he show you? Love...."[45] Somehow, this meaning can be seen only in "... God all-wise our kindly Mother..." who is also, "in this uniting together...our real, true husband."[46] Mother Jesus, He. This paradox is the clue and birth-giver to the meaning, Love, bodied yet shared throughout eternity.

That Dame Julian's Mother Jesus was seen in the body of the Crucified One needs to be set in the larger frame of late medieval devotion to the passion of Jesus Christ. It is on the cross, and in the sacred humanity, which the historian's eye sees as male, that Jesus as Lover and Mother, Priest and Victim at once is met in prayer and sacrament.[47] There are explicit links between devotion to the five wounds and passion of Christ and the later development of the cult of the Sacred Heart of Jesus and the experience of Jesus as the one who embraces as Lover, gives birth from womb/heart (to the world and the individual soul), and nurtures with the blood/water from the wounded side/breasts of his body at Calvary and on the church's altars. So writes Marguerite d'Oingt:

> Ah, who has seen a woman give birth thus!
> And when the hour of birth came, they placed
> You on the bed of the Cross...

And it is not astonishing your veins ruptured, as you gave birth in one single day, to the whole world![48] Carolyn Bynum's work on eucharistic devotion, especially among late medieval women, extends our understanding of how this female/male Jesus shaped real women's lives through ritual and spiritual practice. Bynum suggests that the identification of late medieval women with the nurturing materiality of Jesus, body and sacrament, gave women a literal sensibility of their identity with the humanity of the Son of God which men, "signifying divinity," could not access.[49]

A final text to remind us of this aquifer of hitherto untapped waters takes us back to the early church and *The Acts of the Martyrs of Lyon and Vienne,* A.D. 177. Among those who suffered in the arena on that day was a woman named Blandina:

> Blandina was hung on a post and exposed as bait for the wild animals that were let loose on her. She seemed to hang there in the form of a cross, and by her fervent prayer she aroused intense enthusiasm in those who were undergoing their ordeal, for in their torment with their physical eyes they saw in the person of their sister him who was crucified for them, that he might convince all who believe in him that all who suffer for Christ's glory will have eternal fellowship in the living God.[50]

The passion of the man which disclosed the motherhood of God, here revealed in the witnessing woman the suffering body of God. This, the 1976 Vatican Declaration insists, is impossible![51] It is not just that Jesus, to be proclaimed and seen, must be embodied. It is that "his" body is seen historically as male. But here the symbolic construction of Jesus/God's Body is dis-closed by Blandina's woman-body. "...they saw in the person of their sister him who was crucified..." For the folks to see the woman as a revealer of God, the God who is incarnate must be seen as neither essentially male, nor essentially female, but as both, and therefore as a Third One, who opens the eyes of the beholder to something more than the expected: a torn and dying fanatic named Jesus or Blandina.

The appropriation of patristic or medieval constructions of devotion to the motherhood of God, Jesus, and Mary cannot be simple or straightforward. The milk and blood, plucked from the female pelican, expressed from the breasts of the virgin mother, the experience of spiritual pregnancy, birth and lactation, courtship, marriage and consummation between Jesus and the soul may have been occasions of empowerment and genuine experiences of woman-as-subject for the religious women who report these "shewings" of God infleshed and thus feminized. Contemporary late twentieth century women, Christian or not, will see in the anti-sexual and body-destroying asceticism which too often accompanied this piety no model of the Holy or of the woman-self worth our attention.

These texts are therefore useful only to a point—the point of deconstructing the "simply male" abstract and disembodied imagery and argument of the tradition. For example, Clarissa Atkinson, in her new, exciting and eye-opening book, *The Oldest Vocation, Christian Motherhood in the Middle Ages,* can be read to contextualize the medieval devotion to Jesus Our Mother.[52] Motherhood, in its experienced and idealized twelfth through fourteenth century meanings, involved the inevitability of suffering and the devaluing of all merely human relationships—relationships not only with husbands, but with the worldly "goods" of children also. Hence, the medieval writers found it appropriate to understand God as a mother as well as a son suffering and in self-offering upon the cross. What may be useful for us is not the historically intended meanings of late medieval images of the suffering mother/God—pietà or crucified one, but the way in which gender, and its symbolic freight, whether divine or human, was fluid, unfixed,

and flowing in and out of the social constructions of sex
and gender roles of the culture. Whatever was the symbolized sex of God suffering on the cross, he/she did not simply valorize the patriarchal social order. There is a saving
freedom for us in these gender-bending images, constructed out of the experience of celibate men in same-sex communities and celibate women amid communities of women.

The literary critical paradigm

Marjorie Garber's seriously playful and exhaustive
study, *Vested Interests, Cross-Dressing and Cultural Anxiety* can
provide an exciting and disruptively illuminating
hermeneutic for our task at hand, a Christology which pre-
serves embodiment beyond androcentricity. Garber
believes her interest in cross dressing to be "...an underthe-
orized recognition of the necessary critique of binary
thinking..."[53] One of the most creative contributions of this
work lies in her exploration of what cross-dressing is in its
social-dynamic function. The transvestite (not to be con-
fused with transsexual or homosexual) firstly is a revealer
of the cultural construction of gender categories[54] making
"clear," by the very ambiguity of the presentation, that
gender, to a significant extent, is symbolic and lies in the
eyes of the beholder, who is responding to a set of cultural
clues. This is one of the reasons why Saint Joan of Arc was
finally burned. Her insistence on wearing cross-gender as
well as cross-class (male and knightly garb) was deemed an
unnatural violation of biological and social essentialist definitions of woman. Yet when recognized and canonized as
a saint, her male garb became a symbol of divine vocation!

Transvestites blur and make ambiguous that which
the culture believes it needs to see as a clear and fixed
buffer against unwonted social change. Transvestites
arouse anxiety which comes from encountering people or

things in the wrong place. The transvestite acts like the deacon in brocaded dalmatic who turns out to be a woman (dressed as a man, dressed as a woman) when she starts to sing the Gospel. Jesus acts as a transvestite when he takes a drink from the religiously outcast Samaritan woman or kneels like a slave girl to wash his disciples' feet. Cross-dressing is to indulge in socially taboo behavior. It violates structures and expectations. It de-stabilizes and questions the categories, especially that fundamental duality, male/female.

The cross-dresser is not a "term" in itself, but rather a "disruptive act of putting in question" essences and dualities.[55] What energizes the cross-dresser and destabilizes (sometimes with delight and sometimes with fear and loathing) the on-looker, is to look at the "odd" person or behavior and experience the rush of adrenalin as the categories crumble. The transvestite is a gender-bender, a Third Thing, a person who opens our eyes to "...the permanent crisis of category at the very heart of human culture."[56] We are anxious in her/his presence, for we do not know what to expect, we are out of control. Fluidity replaces stability when gender is unclear. Does the transvestite woman saint participate in, or reveal in some significant way, the gender ambiguity of the Word made Flesh?

Women, seeking God in male clothes, often in response to God, and behaving in what society constructed to be a masculine fashion, seemed more spiritually powerful than the holy men around them. The story handed on is about Pelagia, not about Bishop Nonnus who converted her.[57] In this cross-dressing there was more than a practical arrangement for survival in a men's world. When Perpetua gains a male body, it is more than modesty to protect her spiritual combat from the male gaze of the arena crowds. When Gregory of Nyssa's sister, Macrina, or Jerome's Paula, can no longer be spoken of by her "...natural designation for one who went beyond the nature of a woman,"[58] can such a woman not be called a "Third Thing," one whose power to evangelize and change the world around her is, by virtue of her indubitable womanness, clothed in the mantle of male public strength?

Reconstruction

How can this hermeneutical paradigm be useful to the construction of a feminist Christology? For almost two decades I have asked myself, how can I a woman, find myself, see myself as made in the image of a male God, a God whose human face is seen in the man Jesus? I was excited to discover the pre-Reformation tradition widely sown with female, culturally constructed feminine images for Jesus and his Mother, incarnated quite splendidly in many powerful and socially potent holy women, revered by the culture as saints. But these female namings for the holy were so often limited. They were limited to mother and images of abused and bleeding bodies. These images in our culture can be distressingly negative, as we learn from listening to women's painful memories of "mothering," destructive self-sacrifice, and invasively abused bodies. The mother-naming of God was also often expressed by body-hating and self-abusing women—holy anorectics, women who prayed for the deaths of husband and children. Too frequently the feminine faces of God, especially in God's mother Mary, have been faces of a woman constructed by men for male needs. The work of "unearthing" the female from an androcentric Christian culture must be accompanied by a conscious critique of the cultural construction of motherhood and femininity as found in historical women or the images of God. One has to ask, is Dame Julian's Mother Jesus but one more instance of the male construction of a male god with breasts, another way for the male to "have it all"? Does she point to a world like that wistfully described by Thomas Aquinas, where for all useful activity men serve best—excepting the work of generation and even that birthing can be accomplished by the Son of God?

The paradigm of cross-dressing deconstructs gender essentialism and thus has a hermeneutical potential. Using it we can re-read and un-loose the energies of traditional texts by getting beyond the question of historical "fact" or meaning to recognizing their transgressive and dis-ruptive symbolic potency in the past. This paradigm might well unlock the Jesus women need in our time.

Luce Irigaray writes of this Jesus: "How could 'God' reveal himself in all his magnificence and waste his substance on/in so weak and vile a creature as woman?...It means that love conquers everything that has already been said. And that one man, at least, has understood her so well that he died in the most awful suffering. That most female of men, the Son."[59] By this I would not suggest that Jesus is a "feminine" or androgynous man. Rather, Jesus who was and is both "historical fact" and symbol, a man, is like a "cross-dresser," one not "caught" by the categories. He is a rabbi who drinks and eats with the unclean; he is a preacher of the coming kingdom to Israel who proposes that the uninvited stranger will sit at the feast. He acknowledges his mother and brothers but unravels their family claims and acknowledges sisters and brothers without biological, ethnic or religious boundaries. Even death was, according to the narrative, rent open like the temple veil, not by a ghost, but by one who, embodied (whatever that means, for the category body/spirit is also deconstructed by Jesus), ate and drank and walked through closed doors. We could go on, throughout the Gospel narratives, using Garber's outrageous hermeneutical lens, to see in Jesus the King who died, the man whose life displays "women's ways" of love, sacrifice, and forgiveness, but who was never enclosed by the world's categories. The answer to "what is truth?" lay outside the city walls. And perhaps, as we allow ourselves to be offended by the cross-dressing, we will be able to take seriously that word of Athanasius, "What is not taken up, is not redeemed..." and let Jesus address us as one of her own.

Garber's transvestic phrase, "Third Thing," is a conundrum through which to re-vision the Jesus of ortho-dox Christology, Child of God, a scandal and a stumbling block—the only true God who was also true man, no ordi-nary god, he. Embodied, fleshy, as only a woman in this culture can symbolize, he was a Third Thing, a destroyer of the dualities. In the language of orthodox Christology, he, having broken the crystal wall between the heavens and the earth, was a man, son of Joseph, son of Mary, who was also experienced as Son of God and risen Lord. Truly this was no ordinary man.

Today, in the church and in the culture, it is not the divine/human dichotomy but gender which is the para-digm of crisis. Responding to this holy opportunity, this Christology invites a re-vision of Jesus Christ understood and prayed to with these transvestic sensibilities. Jesus is the Trickster who peels us open to new depths of humani-ty, divinity, femaleness, maleness. There might be no telling what boundaries and categories could be dis-man-tled as male gender hegemony is disrobed. That is what the Gospel is about, the piercing of categories in the womb/by the dart of Love. A merely male Jesus has been and continues to be a violation of the scandal and trans-gression which is the Gospel.

The reconstructed experience

The priest is not the same as the Reformed pastor, preacher of the bare Word. The woman-priest stands at the altar, no matter what her theology of ordination, *in persona Christi.* She symbolizes "body" by her very womanness, and when as a priest, she handles, "makes," God's Body, she stands for the crucified Jesus of the tradition, giving birth to transformed and redeemed creation. To appreciate how repulsive this "acted out Christology" is in an androcentric and misogynist church and society there is no need to cite learned articles. Look simply at the extraordinary resistance in the Anglican Communion and the increasingly frantic opposition to any hint of ordaining women in both Roman Catholicism and the Orthodox churches. The "woman dressed as a man dressed as a woman"[60] is a cross-dresser, "shaking the foundations" with the transgressive energy of the taboo gesture, a woman's body in a sacred space, mediating, as a representative parson, God. She literally flies in the face of culture and classical Christology according to which only a man can be a representative person whether Christ or priest.

And, it is very likely that with time, congregations who gather in sacramental celebration with such women will be experiencing Jesus differently. Women are in the arena, and like Blandina, their woman-ways of bodied being evoke the experience in those around them, of "...seeing with their physical eyes...in her, Him who was crucified for them...." When the icons we use to mediate the holy are women, we will see Jesus to be a her, like us. We will be like the lion who leaped with excited confirmation when Aslan said "us lions." It will be a long time before that blurring of boundary which is a promised sign of the reign of God will be greeted with ease and relief. We are still resistant to the other. Witness the threat which a black Jesus or a mother or lover Jesus presents to normative male, white humanity with its transcendent distinctions, anti-eroticism, and carefully delineated gender privilege. Children will have to be raised differently—fathered as intimately as mothered. All this does not happen in church, nor in a re-visioned Christology. Yet supported by "cross-dressed" models, Christians will be called to break repressive convention. The Blandinas and Pelagias and St. Joans of the tradition and women in whom the sacred is met in dailyness will enable the world to see and sense experience topsy-turvy, evangelically. The dualities will be broken, profane and holy, law and love, death and life, just as they were in the Garden. Christians believe in a Jesus "dressed" in flesh, that most female of symbols, and they believe in a God in man-flesh who behaves like a woman. This "transvestite" Jesus makes a human space where no one is out of place because the notion of place and gender has been transformed. Yes human, yes god, yes woman, yes man, yes black, yes white, yes yellow, yes friend, yes stranger...yes, yes, yes.

Notes

1. This is a condensed version of "Feminist Christologies: Bodies and Boundaries," in Robert Berkey and Sarah Edwards, eds., *Christology in Dialogue* (New York: Pilgrim Press, forthcoming).

2. C.S. Lewis, *The Lion, The Witch and The Wardrobe* (New York: Macmillan, 1950), 142.

3. Unpublished working paper, Irenaeus Fellowship of Bishops of the Episcopal Church, U.S.A., 1991.

4. Daphne Hampson, *Theology and Feminism* (Oxford: Basil Blackwell, 1990), 71. Hampson remarks that as a Christian feminist, she had no interest in the gender of Christ, female symbols of the Holy, or "inclusive language."

5. Richard Norris, "The Ordination of Women and the 'Maleness' of Christ," *Anglican Theological Revue,* Supplementary Series 6 (June, 1976): 69-80.

6. John Macquarrie, *Jesus Christ in Modern Thought* (London: SCM Press, 1990), 359-60.

7. E.L. Mascall, quoted in Michael Bruce and G.E. Duffield, eds. *Why Not? Priesthood and the Ministry of Women* (United Kingdom: Appleford Publishing Group, 1972), 111-12.

8. *Book of Common Prayer,* 423.

9. From a speech by Bishop Graham Leonard to the General Synod of the Church of England, Nov. 8, 1978 (The Church Literature Association for the Church Union), cited in Hampson, *Theology,* see n. 4 above, 66.

10. Macquarrie, *Jesus Christ,* see n. 6 above, 6.

11. Macquarrie, *Jesus Christ,* see n. 6 above, 12.

12. Macquarrie, *Jesus Christ,* see n. 6 above, 302.

13. Macquarrie, *Jesus Christ,* see n. 6 above, 316. Here Macquarrie affirmatively cites Jon Sabrino, *Christology at the Crossroads* (Maryknoll, NY: Orbis Press, 1978), 379.

14. Macquarrie, *Jesus Christ,* see n. 6 above, 9, in J.D.G Dunn, *Unity and Diversity in the New Testament: An Inquiry into the Character of Earliest Christianity* [?] (Philadelphia: Westminster, 1977), 376.

15. See Hampson, *Theology,* see note 4 above, 65, where, for example, she dismisses Rosemary Ruether as a humanist.

16. Carter Heyward, *The Redemption of God, A Theology of Mutual Relation* (Lanham, MD: United Press of America, 1982), 196.

17. See Hampson, *Theology,* n. 4 above, 61, where she seems to make too sharp a distinction between historical "fact" and symbol, as if the historical "fact" of the maleness of Jesus does not function as a symbol; giving priority to historical "fact" as "true" in a way that symbol is not.

18. See Hampson, *Theology,* n. 4 above, 50. Hampson defines feminism as an extension of Enlightenment equality to women.

19. Elaine Pagels, *The Gnostic Gospels* (New York: Random House, 1979).

20. Heyward, *Redemption,* see n. 16 above, 185-86.

21. Macquarrie, *Jesus Christ,* see n. 16 above, 16, citing Martin Kaehler, *The So-called Historical Jesus and Historic Biblical Christ* (Philadelphia: Fortress, 1964), 66.

22. Jacquelyne Grant, *White Women's Christ and Black Women's Jesus, Feminist Christology and Womanist Response* (Atlanta: Scholars Press, 1989), 144., "...the maleness of Jesus is superseded by the Christness of Jesus."

23. Grant, *White Women's Christ,* see n. 22 above, 215-16. "The identification is so real that Jesus Christ in fact becomes black."

24. *The New York Times,* April 27, 1984. "...Bishop Dennis said he did not object to "enhancing" symbols of Jesus by casting them in different skin colors or ethnic characteristics. But he said the statue went too far by "totally changing the symbol."

25. Marjorie Hewitt Suchocki, *God Christ Church, A Practical Guide to Process Theology* (New York: Crossroad, 1982), 104.

26. Carter Heyward, *Touching Our Strength, The Erotic as Power and the Love of God* (New York: Harper, 1989); Paul Avis, *Eros and the Sacred* (Harrisburg, PA: Morehouse, 1990); Alexander C. Irwin, *Eros Toward the World: Paul Tillich and the Theology of the Erotic* (Minneapolis: Fortress, 1991).

27. Avis, *Eros,* see n. 26 above, 128-137.

28. See Irenaeus Fellowship of Bishops, "A Theological Critique of the Human Sexuality and Environment" Sections of the Standing Commission on Human Affairs Report to the 70th General Convention of the Episcopal Church, 5 where the (unsigned) Episcopal authors attack the work of Sallie McFague and Carter Heyward as holding a too intimate connection between Creator and Creation, teaching an embodied divinity which fails to honor the dualities between fallen world and good God.

29. Cited in Kenneth Leech, *True Prayer* (New York: Harper, 1980), 9.

30. Cited in Hampson, *Theology,* see n. 4 above, 33.

31. See for example, how the "body" of lay Christians is always represented as the female bride of Christ, the Church, subordinate and obedient to her bridegroom; how the female body is used in advertising to represent and arouse the response of male desire; how the earth has "breast" and the wind, "voice."

32. André Cabassut, *Revue d'ascetique et de mystique*

25(1949): 234-45. I am indebted to Prof. Giles Constable, then at Harvard University, for this reference.

33. Eleanor McLaughlin, "Christ my Mother: Feminine Naming and Metaphor in Medieval Spirituality," *Nashotah Review* 15, no. 3 (Fall, 1975), 228-248.

34. Caroline Bynum, "...and Woman His Humanity: Female Imagery in the Religious Writing of the Later Middle Ages," *Fragmentation and Redemption, Essays on Gender and the Human Body in Medieval Religion* (New York: Urzone, 1991), 151-71.

35. Janet Martin Soskice, *Metaphor and Religious Language* (Oxford: Clarendon, 1987), 160.

36. Clement of Alexandria, "Christ the Educator," *The Fathers of the Church,* v. 23 (New York: Fathers of the Church, 1954), I:43, I:42, 40-41. It may be because in "that other world," the "...human person [is] freed from the lust that in life had made it either male or female" (I:10), that God the Father may be seen as equipped with breasts and "...it is more than evident that the Blood of Christ is milk." (I:40)

37. Caroline Walker Bynum, "Jesus as Mother and Abbot as Mother: Some Themes in Twelfth-Century Cistercian Writing," *Jesus as Mother, Studies in the Spirituality of the High Middle Ages* (Berkeley: University of California, 1982), 110-169.

38. Sister Benedicta Ward, ed. and trans., *The Prayers and Meditations of Saint Anselm* (Harmondsworth: Penguin, 1973), 124.

39. Ward, *Saint Anselm,* see n. 38 above, 155-6.

40. Ward, *Saint Anselm,* see n. 38 above, 154.

41. Julian of Norwich, *Revelations of Divine Love,* ed. Clifton Wolters (Harmondsworth: Penguin, 1973), ch. 13, 84.

42. Julian, *Revelations,* see n. 41 above, ch. 60; 170.

43. Julian, *Revelations,* see n. 41 above, ch. 9, 10; 76.

44. Julian, *Revelations,* see n. 41 above, ch. 52; 152.

45. Julian, *Revelations,* see n. 41 above, ch. 86; 211.

46. Julian, *Revelations,* see n. 41 above, ch. 58; 165.

47. "...he openeth them as doth the mother her arms to embrace her beloved child.... And thou, dear Lord, goest spiritually toward us and to thy darlings with the same embrace as the

mother to her children." *Ureisan of Ure Louerde*, ed. W. Meredith Thompson (London: Early English Text Society, 241, 1958), cited in John Bugge, *Virginitas: An Essay on the History of a Medieval Ideal* (The Hague: Martinus Nijhoff, 1975), 100. Bugge speaks of the "disquieting phenomenon" of the shift in the metaphorical sexuality of Christ from male to female. What he finds disquieting, I find central to the transvestic quality of Incarnation.

48. McLaughlin, "Christ my Mother," 235, citing A. Duraffour, P. Gardette and P. Durdilly, *Les Oeuvres de Marguerite d'Oingt* (Parish, 1965), 33-36.

49. Bynum, "...and Woman His Humanity," see n. 34 above, 179: "...religious women...understood that 'man...signifies the divinity of the Son of God and woman his humanity.' And they understood that both equations were metaphorical. But, given the ultimate dichotomy of God and creation, the first was only metaphorical. Man was not divinity. The second was in some sense, however, literally true."

50. Herbert Musurillo, *The Acts of the Christian Martyrs* (Oxford: Clarendon, 1972), 75.

51. Congregation for the Doctrine of the Faith, *Inter Insigniores*, Declaration on the Question of Admission of Women to the Ministerial Priesthood (Washington, D.C.: U.S.C.C., 1976).

52. Clarissa Atkinson, *The Oldest Vocation, Christian Motherhood in the Middle Ages* (Ithaca, NY: Cornell, 1991). Atkinson is interested in what devotional materials can tell us about the social construction of human motherhood. I am particularly interested to develop theologically her identification of the shift from the valorizing of virginity in the Catholic centuries to the Protestant sacralizing of the heterosexual, patriarchal family. It is my thesis that the masculinization of God accompanies and perhaps contributes to this shift.

53. Marjorie Garber, *Vested Interests, Cross-Dressing and Cultural Anxiety* (New York: Routledge, Chapman and Hall, 1992), 10-11.

54. Garber, *Vested Interests,* see n. 53 above, 9.

55. Garber, *Vested Interests,* see n. 53 above, 12.

56. Garber, *Vested Interests,* see n. 53 above, 16.

57. Benedicta Ward, *Harlots of the Desert, A Study of Repentance in Early Monastic Sources* (Kalamazoo: Cistercian Publications, 1987), 66-75.

58. Gregory of Nyssa, *Life of St. Macrina* (The Fathers of the Church, v. 58 (New York: The Fathers of the Church, 1954), 163.

59. Luce Irigaray, *Speculum of the Other Woman* (Ithaca, NY: Cornell), 199.

60. Eleanor McLaughlin, "The Gendered Priest and the Passions and Parts of God" (Paper delivered at the Johnson Lectures, Seabury Western Theological School, October, 1987).

Contributors

Rosemary Radford Ruether, author of some twenty-two books and many articles, holds the Georgia Harkness Professorship in Pastoral Theology at Garrett-Evangelical Theological Seminary in Evanston, Illinois. In addition she is a regular columnist for the *National Catholic Reporter* and a contributing editor for *Christianity and Crisis* and *The Journal of Religion and Intellectual Life.* In 1983 she was hailed as U.S. Catholic of the Year by *U.S. Catholic.* Dr. Ruether's latest book is an edited collection titled *A Democratic Catholic Church: The Reconstruction of Roman Catholicism.*

Rita Nakashima Brock is an Associate Professor in the Endowed Chair in the Humanities at Hamline University, St. Paul, Minnesota. Her book, *Journeys By Heart: A Christology of Erotic Power,* won the 1988 Crossroad/Continuum Press Award for the most outstanding manuscript in Women's Studies. She was a member of the Board of the Center for the Prevention of Sexual and Domestic Violence in Seattle, Washington, from 1989-1990 and currently sits on the editorial board of the *Journal of Feminist Studies in Religion.* Dr. Brock has published a number of essays on feminist theology, peace, and Asian American women's theology.

Jacquelyn Grant is Associate Professor in Systematic Theology at the Interdenominational Theological Center in Atlanta, Georgia. Her book, *White Women's Christ and Black Women's Jesus: Feminist Christology and Womanist Response,* argues that Christology is simply irrelevant if it does not take into account the black experience of struggle against oppression. Dr. Grant is an ordained elder in the African Methodist Episcopal tradition, and during the 1991-92 academic year she was the first to hold the the Willa B. Player Endowed Chair in the Humanities at Bennett College in Greensboro, North Carolina.

Marina Herrera is a lecturer in the Missiology department at the Washington Theological Union, Washington, D.C. Dr. Herrera conducts workshops on planning and developing strategies for intercultural communication and celebration in educational and religious settings. She was also a consultant to the National Conference of Catholic Bishops Fifth Centenary Committee on the pastoral *Heritage and Hope,* and she authored an education guide on the quincentenary for Catholic school students, *The Cross: Our Heritage and Our Hope.*

Elizabeth A. Johnson is Associate Professor of Theology at Fordham University, Bronx, New York. In addition to numerous articles, she has published two books: *Consider Jesus: Waves of Renewal in Christology,* and *She Who Is: A Feminist Theology of God.* In addition, Dr. Johnson is a member of the national U.S. Lutheran/Roman Catholic Dialogue and a member of the advisory board for the National Conference of Catholic Bishops Committee on Women in Church and Society.

Eleanor McLaughlin is currently writing a book on feminist Christology while a research associate at the Five College Women's Studies Center in South Hadley, Massachusetts. Combining her scholarly and pastoral interests, Dr. McLaughlin lectures and publishes on a wide variety of topics using medieval spirituality as her focus. She also currently serves as assisting priest at Grace Episcopal Church in Amherst, Massachusetts.